READ IT
and
WIPE

Condensed Comedy for the Can

By Justin Heimberg
and David Gomberg

Published by Seven Footer Press
276 Fifth Ave., Suite 301
New York, NY 10001

First Printing, January 2009
10 9 8 7 6 5 4 3 2

Design by Junko Miyakoshi

ISBN-13 978-1-934734-10-0

www.sevenfooterpress.com

WHAT PEOPLE ARE SAYING ABOUT

Read It and Wipe!!!

"I don't have time to read it. I'm sorry."
— JOYCE CAROL OATES

"You'll have to talk to my publicist."
— PHILIP ROTH

"I'm sorry. Mr. Roth is not doing blurbs right now."
— PHILIP ROTH'S Publicist

"I cannot help you."
— JOHN UPDIKE

"My publicist handles these types of requests."
— SALMAN RUSHDIE

"We can't help you with that.... I'm sorry to hear that
it's hard to get— ... I am sympathetic...
Well then, maybe you should take a break."
— SALMAN RUSHDIE'S Publicist

"So, that's a large cheese and two Cokes?"
— MILT, Beach Pizza

"Read it and what?... Are you kidding me?
Mr. Kundera writes serious fiction...
He has no interest in this garbage....
No, he doesn't have a story about having diarrhea in public.
...well, not one he wants to share."
— MILAN KUNDERA'S Publicist

"I'm sorry... What do you want me to do about it?...
You suck... No you suck... No, you suck!...
You suck infinity plus one."
— HIS HOLINESS, THE DALAI LAMA,
Author of The Art of Happiness

"Just calm down. I know it's a lonely profession,
but don't do anything rash. Think of the people
who love you. Be persistent. Don't give up."
— DR. MORT FRIEDMAN, Ph.D, LSW

"No, I said... I know you are but what am I...
Well then, step up!... Take your balls out of your purse...
You suck... You suck!... Shut your trap before
I open up a can of Tibetan whoop-ass on you."
— HIS HOLINESS, THE DALAI LAMA,
Author of The Art of Happiness

"These blurbs are not real. We'd like to make that legal disclamer."
— LEN STEIN, Attorney for Mr. Heimberg and Mr. Gomberg

INTRODUCTION

Read It and Wipe!!!

The bathroom book is a most underappreciated art form. Many of history's great writers eventually embraced the literary potential of potty reading: Shakespeare, for example, cut his plays down to one-session sized sonnets. Likewise, the Bible came out with the more quickly digestible Psalms. Both were perfectly abbreviated for an excretory excursion.

Every ensuing great artist has sought to meet the challenge: The Great American Bathroom Book must entertain or inform in—forgive the phrasing—short bursts. And in the case of the comedic bathroom book, the material must quickly induce laughter, and yet not such laughter as to adversely affect the bowel movement in process.

The Great American Bathroom Book should have pieces of different length to reflect the length of a respective bowel movement—let me rephrase that—to reflect the respective duration of a bowel movement.

Subject matter is just as important as format. Studies indicate that what you read while on the throne can have a profound effect on your personality. For example, recently I put a vocabulary builder on the back of my toilet. When one learns new words or a new idea, it is the mind's natural inclination to process and remember the words and ideas in the context of the learning environment. Consequently, I have become an extremely interesting and articulate party guest—but only in the context of describing my BMs. Just the other night over cocktails, I regaled a table full of my fellow writers and artists with a charming description of my "bacchanalian fecal deposits, a cornucopia of fetid iniquity."

From this, a great lesson was learned: the subject matter of the Great American Bathroom Book should be light: funny, occasionally informative, easily processed. James Joyce is not meant to be read on the toilet, bless him for trying. One should not have to grimace and grunt in concentration—there is enough of that going on anyway.

A reasonable defecation provides peace, if only for a moment, a respite from the concerns and obligations of adult life. Put another way: no one can give you shit while you're taking one. This time is yours alone. So go on, gentle reader, read the silliness, enjoy the fun and games, purge your mind of all the concerns and responsibilities on the "outside." Enjoy the catharsis. It's one colossal braindump. Read it and wipe.

Sincerely,

Justin Heimberg
Ph.D, Scatology

How to Use This Book

We've organized this book into four parts: **Short Bursts, Medium Bits, Long Pieces**, and **The Diarrhea Monologues**. That way, as you begin your endeavor you can make an estimate of how long your pit stop will be and choose a piece, or pieces, of appropriate length. Match the material to your movement like a fine wine to a meal.

Spotted amidst the bits of various lengths are kernels (undigested) of **Toilet Trivia** (facts about your body, its bodily functions, and bathroom history) and other features such as **When the Ball Drops**: personal and true accounts of having diarrhea pangs (or worse) in public places, and the drama that ensues.

THE DOODIE LOG

We would be remiss not to mention the **Doodie Log**. You'll find it at the end of the book and it's the place where you and your guests can leave your mark in signature, name, and overall description of the experience. There are few experiences in life more intimate than sharing this magical act. It brings the world together. Imagine.

Lastly, we've provided some **Emergency Toilet Paper** at the end of the book for the worst case scenario. (Make sure to read the instructions before using.)

SHORT BURSTS

WHEN THE BALL DROPS
Great Stories in Diarrhea

at the moment of reckoning,

when there is no tomorrow or yesterday,

when the cork comes out of the bottle...

...the ball drops.

⚠ Shaky Landing ⚠

I was on a plane and the "fasten seatbelt" light came on as we began our descent. For the last hour or so I had been holding in a big crap, debating whether the pressure warranted relieving. I really didn't want to go on the plane. As a guy, I wasn't so concerned with the germs, but I've always had a fear of that weird, violent airplane bathroom toilet flush (I once heard a story about some guy's intestines being ripped from his body as he flushed). I decided to tempt fate and hold it.

By the time we touched down, I was about to burst. I was sitting in one of the back rows and it was pure torture waiting for the logjam in the aisle to start moving. Passengers took their sweet time, leisurely removing their luggage and sauntering down the aisle. It didn't look like I was going to make it so I took matters into my own hands. I nearly knocked an old woman down as I hurried through the jetway into the airport and dashed into the first bathroom I could find.

Just as I was about to lose control of my sphincter, I darted into a stall, dropped my pants and sat down in one motion, and let it rip with a cacophony of farts, grunts, and fecal debris. Just as an amazing sense of relief set in, I looked down to see a pair of high heels in the stall next to me. I had run into the women's bathroom. —TD

The Birthday

"Can I have a doggy for my birthday, please?" The request was constantly pleaded by little Cedrick. He desperately wanted a dog. His parents wanted to give him a dog, but just couldn't afford one. They felt so sad. But suddenly, Cedrick's parents had an idea... On Cedrick's birthday, he was greeted by a cute, furry little creature. Cedrick's eyes widened and tears flowed from them—not from joy but from pain. Cedrick's idiotic parents had caught a wild raccoon and stapled some floppy, cardboard ears on it too make it look like a dog. The incensed raccoon immediately bit little Cedrick, forcing him to undergo a series of painful rabies shots. This was the worst birthday ever.

Facts That Sound For a Second Like They Might Be True But Aren't

Women originally wore make-up for warmth.

The giraffe is the only other species that engages in masturbation.

Ben Franklin invented an early version of Pringles.

In 1938, "Milt" was the most popular name for both men and women.

There's a tribe in the Amazon that never cuts the umbilical cord.

Earth is the only planet named after a Jew.

The dishwasher was invented by accident.

A tortoise can sustain an erection for seven and a half years.

Scotch tape is so named because it originally had traces of scotch on the sticky side for flavor.

More people are killed each year by luggage carts than in plane crashes.

Michael Jackson took his patented moonwalk move from General Custer.

Jesus had Tourette's Syndrome.

TOILET TRIVIA

The composition of a typical poop is 75% water, 8% dead bacteria, 8% fiber, and 8% fats, phosphates, protein, bacteria, and other goodies.

Would you rather...

ORGASM ONCE
EVERY 20 YEARS

ONCE EVERY 20 SECONDS?

WATCH A PORNO MOVIE
WITH YOUR PARENTS

WATCH A PORNO MOVIE
STARRING YOUR PARENTS?

Are you as ethical as you think?
Read the question below and see how you
deal with a difficult moral dilemma.

An unbelievably attractive spouse of a close friend offers you the chance for a one-time "no one will know" affair. Do you partake in oral or anal sex?

You are walking down the street when you see someone drop a hundred dollar bill and walk off obliviously. Do you spend the money on whores or crack?

A social agency wants to establish a residence for seven retarded adults next door to your house. Another neighbor has written up a petition against the home and asks you to sign. Do you dominate the retards in basketball or football?

You're attractive, but poor and without skills. Someone offers you lots of money to work for an escort service. How can I get in touch with you?

You're buying a house from an old lady. She's asking a price that is way too low. Do you partake in oral or anal sex?

THIS *OR* THAT?

Famous Children's Book or Infamous Nazi Nickname?

a. The Desert Fox

b. The Velveteen Rabbit

c. Beppo

d. The Lorax

e. The Blonde Beast

f. The Blue Man

g. Globus

h. The Iron Man

i. Super Fudge

a. Nazi. The Desert Fox was Erwin Rommel.
b. Children's Book. The Velveteen Rabbit by Margery Williams.
c. Nazi. Beppo was Josef Mengele.
d. Children's Book. The Lorax by Dr. Seuss.
e. Nazi. The Blond Beast was Reinhard Heydrich.
f. Children's Book. The Blue Man by Kin Platt.
g. Nazi. Globus was Odilo Globocnik.
h. Children's Book. The Iron Man by Ted Hughes.
i. Children's Book. Super Fudge by Judy Blume.

 Unlikely Novelizations

Pac-Man: The Novel

Ever-chomping, Pac-Man fled, his mind a blur of dots and darkness. He was operating on instinct now, navigating the labyrinthine hell with a madness to match the situation. Blinky pursued, undead and pastel, the blank look in his eyes belying his thirst for death. And then, in an instant, it all changed. Night was day. Light was dark. For the gluttonous refugee had reached his engorged spheroid goal, and just like that, the chaser had become the chasee.

Vocabulary
Builder

Brought to you by Classless Education, making learning bearable since 2007

Yo momma's so **unctuous**, her freckles slipped off.

unc·tu·ous (UNGK choo uhs)

adj. Having an oily or soapy feel; excessively smooth, suave, or smug; having the quality or characteristics of oil or ointment; slippery

Unctuous can mean slippery or oily (if you're an oyster lover, it's the perfect word to describe them), but it is generally used to describe a person who is excessively smooth, someone who radiates insincere earnestness. Con artists are unctuous, used car salesmen are as unctuous as the cars they wax, and politicians are too often the apotheosis (see p.51) of unctuousness. People's love-hate opinion of President Bill Clinton speaks to the fine subjective line between sincerity and unctuousness. Did he really feel our pain? Unctuous people are just too polished and ingratiating to trust. Think of Ryan Seacrest asking innocuous, you're-my-pal questions to "*American Idol*" contestants, or, perhaps more accurately, the wannabe managers fawning over the finalists of the show, hoping to represent them as they sign big label deals.

🔫 Bad James Bond Villainess Names:

- ✻ Kopi Osbuti
- ✻ Cindy Mons Pubis
- ✻ Extrava Gantlabia
- ✻ Polly Orchid
- ✻ Knockers Franklin

🧍Pornification🧍

For every movie, there exists, at least theoretically, a porno version of that movie. Can you "pornify" the titles below?

The Nutty Professor

Cold Mountain

Malcolm X

Space Jam

Glory

Big Trouble in Little China

Pearl Harbor

You've Got Mail

Gladiator

Dirty Harry

(Answers on page 10)

TOILET TRIVIA

Added all together, the average American spends three years on the toilet.

Pornification

(Answer Key for the quiz on page 9)

The Nutty Professor = The Slutty Professor

Cold Mountain = Cold Mountin'

Malcolm X = Malcolm XXX

Space Jam = Face Jam

Glory = Glory Hole

Big Trouble in Little China = Big Trouble in Little Vagina

Pearl Harbor = Pearl Necklace

You've Got Mail = You've Got She-male

Gladiator = Glad-he-ate-her

Dirty Harry = Dirty, Harry

7 Things You Never Want to Hear

1. "No, that was an anal thermometer."

2. "Is this your skin?"

3. "Turns out religion *is* important."

4. "I now pronounce you Mr. and Mrs. Basedow."

5. "A new study reports scratching yourself causes cancer."

6. "Prepare to be fisted."

7. "Oh yes, athlete's foot can spread to other parts of your body."

How Would Seuss Say It

"I'm sorry, sir. You have six months to live."

Your heart is a pumping

Your heart is a popping

But one year in half

Your heart will be stopping

It'll clonk, it'll clank

It'll cloink, it'll clunk

And then your body will fall

Just like that—kerplunk!

And you'll be tossed in the ground

With all sorts of junk.

TOILET TRIVIA

Famous people who died on the toilet include author Evelyn Waugh, comedian Lenny Bruce, producer Don Simpson, and five kings (Edmund II, James I, Henry III, George II, and Elvis Presley).

Yo-Yo Ma Jokes

Yo-Yo Ma is so fat, he has to hold his breath to play his cello!

Yo-Yo Ma's teeth so crooked he can floss with his bow. SNAP!

Yo-Yo Ma is so old, he played live accompaniment for Schubert! Schubert, fool!

Yo-Yo Ma is so stupid he took his cello in to get it fixed because they told him it was Baroque!

Yo-Yo Ma is so fat, when he sits down, the orchestra skips! Aw Damn!

Yo-Yo Ma's so stupid he thought "crescendos" were part of a nutritious breakfast!

Yo-Yo Ma's breath so stank, if he played the bassoon, he'd melt it.

———— Alternative ways to answer ———— in the form of a question on *Jeopardy!*

How bout' a little bit of _____?

Who's your _____?

Am I just dripping with ecstasy as I answer _____ or what?

Is that a _____ in your pants or are you just happy to see me?

You want me to say _____, don't you?

Should I kick your face in or is it_____?

WHEN THE BALL DROPS
Great Stories in Diarrhea

at the moment of reckoning,

when there is no tomorrow or yesterday,

when the cork comes out of the bottle...

...the ball drops.

⚠ MacGyver and Me ⚠

I'll bet you've never sharted yourself in Bloomingdale's while holding your girlfriend's pocketbook as she was trying something on, but sadly, I have. Luckily, I did this a few weeks after receiving a Swiss Army knife keychain as a gift. It would turn out to be a gift from heaven. Once the accident happened, I waddled over to the changing room where I informed my girlfriend that she needed to hold her "own damn pocketbook for a few minutes." She sensed my desperation, knew my propensity for soiling myself, and cut me free. After what can only be described as moonwalking on my heels, I made it to the bathroom. I tried to look cool in the crowd. I sashayed over to the toilet with the grace of a millionaire trying on brand new clothes. But now I had another problem: the restroom was crowded and I didn't want any of the assembled shoppers to see me throwing the evidence into the trash.

I went into a stall, sat down on the toilet (with many layers of padding) and thought about what to do. Then I remembered: I had my Swiss Army knife keychain! I proceeded to cut my underwear off myself like an EMT. I sliced my shitstained drawers into strips and flushed them down the toilet like I was Mac-Gyver dissembling a bomb, just in time to save the world. After that, I guess I was just like any other dude walking around Bloomingdale's with no underwear on. —JM

MindF*cks:
9 Things to Do at a Job Interview to Screw with the Interviewer

1. At the top of your resume, print (in italics) song lyrics that inspire you, such as:

> *I'd die for you, you know it's true*
> *Everything I do—I do it for you*
> —*Bryan Adams (from* Robin Hood, Prince of Thieves*)*

2. Smell your fingers periodically.

3. Quote Jesus a little too often.

4. Ask for a ride home.

5. Refer to yourself several times as a "grown-ass man", as in "I don't need micromanaging. I'm a grown-ass man."

6. Bring an "attorney" to your interview. Consult the attorney whenever you're asked a question, and have the attorney whisper to you before answering.

7. Wink frequently.

8. Bring a pocket dictionary. Every time the interviewer mentions a mildly sophisticated word, open the dictionary, look up the word, repeat the definition quietly, and then close the dictionary and answer the question normally.

9. List all of your references as "(Deceased.)"

13 Terrible First Sentences for a Novel

1. The pudding seemed to breathe.

2. Klarence liked his women like he liked his kickball pitches—slow and smooth.

3. Barney stood proudly in his lemon-peel pants.

4. She was all ligaments.

5. The pilgrim's orgy was a disaster.

6. Before going in, Larry put his underpants over his fist.

7. Elegar the Druid plunged his +5 Doom Broad Sword (transferring) into the barked neck of Lezzen the Orc Prince as Shelby the Bloated watched from the dark pools, molting like there was no tomorrow.

8. Needledorf was his name; Needledorf, by coincidence, was also his game.

9. The joy in his heart spread like athlete's foot (spreads).

10. The sun set downward.

11. The truth hit him like a kick to the vagina.

12. "Lugnuts, anyone?" she asked, surreptitiously.

13. Nils's scrotum ballooned.

Dorfman

Everyone hates being sick. Everyone that is except for Dorfman. While others cry or moan when they are sick, Dorfman would holler for joy. One year, he wasn't sick once and he started to cry. But then a smile came to Dorfman's face. He realized he *was* sick. He was mentally ill!

Too Tall Sharon

Sharon was too tall. For years, she had grown and grown and grown. Now she was six-foot four. Sharon felt bad and cried. Until one day, she tried out for the girl's basketball team. Although she was six-foot four, the coach said she had never seen "such a pathetic waste of height ... such a lack of talent and skill." Sharon became a whore.

WHEN THE BALL DROPS
Great Stories in Diarrhea

at the moment of reckoning,

when there is no tomorrow or yesterday,

when the cork comes out of the bottle...

...the ball drops.

⚠ The Fish Shit In Here Too ⚠

When I was a kid in sleepaway camp, there was a huge emphasis on passing a particular lifeguard safety test. The test wasn't easy. A big part of it involved treading water for what felt like a day, but was actually only an hour. This camp didn't have very good food. One day I was treading water next to a kid who told me his stomach hurt. Fearing the worst, I treaded further away. He warned me that he didn't know if he could hold it much longer. I told him, "Get the fuck out of the lake and take a shit."

"I can't," he replied, "I'm past the point of no return."

I swam away as if fleeing from an atomic explosion. I heard him shout in the distance, "Besides, it's a fucking lake and the fish shit in here too."
And then he let it rip. Since then, I don't feel so guilty when I pee in the ocean.
—JM

TOILET TRIVIA

The first recorded use of a flush toilet occurred during the reign of King Minos on the island of Crete circa 1700 BC.

How Would Seuss Say It

"I just don't love you anymore"

I do not love you anymore

I do not love you when you snore

I do not love you in the sack

I do not love you with a yak

I do not love you on a plane

I do not love you in the rain

I do not love you in sleet or snow

I do not love you when barometric pressure is low

I do not love you in the fall

I do not love you under any meteorological conditions at all

I do not love you in the car

I do not love you with Jamie Farr

I do not love you on Yom Kippur

I just don't love you anymore

Not in the leastest the very most leastest

The lesser then least of the very most leastest

There's nothing for me to love you for

I just don't love you anymore

Would you rather...

HAVE MONOPOLY HOTEL
AND HOUSES BOOGERS

DEFECATE RUBIK'S SNAKES?

BE BLUDGEONED TO DEATH
WITH A SLAB OF BEEF

BE TRAPPED IN A SUBMARINE
UNTIL IT SLOWLY FILLED UP
WITH ELVIS IMPERSONATORS?

www.wouldyourather.com

Emixocillyn 9

The makers of Emixocillyn 9 are not responsible for anything that happens as a result of this drug, or anything else in your life. By informing you of the possible side effects shown from the drug's history, the makers are indemnified from any possible charges. Side effects of Emixocillyn 9: 85% of those previously tested experienced eye discomfort, 83% experienced sporadic drowsiness, 77% became obsessed with anything brown, 73% could no longer differentiate between urinals and family members, 69% experienced loss/acquisition of limbs, 67% began to tell the punchlines of jokes in Arabic, 49% began to regularly use the word "tugboat" as a verb. 43% developed a strange green mark on their backs that looked not entirely unlike Gabe Kaplan. 28% became preoccupied with the thought that "clapping your hands if you're happy and you know it" is redundant and unnecessary if "your face will surely show it." 26% could no longer comprehend any written material save Apartment 3-G comics. 24% experienced a hair transformation wherein their hair increasingly resembled the mane of the Reverend Al Sharpton. 18% of volunteers' navels migrated to their back. 15% could no long successfully pronounce the word "milkweed." (Substitutes included "miltworl" and "klinsorn.") .00001% have been mysteriously stalked by former Senator Alan Cranston (causality not confirmed.), 43% made the sound of shaking Boggle letter cubes any time they attempted to speak, 34% developed a quarterback-like compulsion to lick throwing hand's thumb, 8% wandered aimlessly searching for the little "gnomes who have come to steal the puddings," 23% broke out with an Orion constellation of warts, 20% experienced burning sensation when they urinated, 34% experienced mawkish nostalgia about the Scottish countryside when they urinated, 56% vomited dice, 12% excreted monopoly real estate, 19% reenacted the battle of Hastings repeatedly until exhausted, 100% waxed indignantly about Felton Spencer, 6% began chillin' like a villain, 7% developed moth-producing yawns, 5% melted, 3% malted, 1% molted, 31% lost all sexual inhibition in front of C.P.A.'s.

WHEN THE BALL DROPS
Great Stories in Diarrhea

at the moment of reckoning,
when there is no tomorrow or yesterday,
when the cork comes out of the bottle...

...the ball drops.

⚠ Backyard Blues 1 ⚠

I was only 4 years old and was playing in the woods. Nature called and I ran back home to take a deuce, but couldn't make it so I squatted in our neighbor's yard. When my innocent little face looked up, I realized the whole family was on the back porch eating dinner, looking down at me. To this day, whenever I meet the dad of that family, I see in his eyes a look that says, "You're the f-ing kid who took a shit in my yard." —KG

⚠ Picture Perfect ⚠

A old friend was over and for fun, we decided to look at old photos, from well before the pre-digital era. So each of us has a stack we're rifling through, and suddenly my friend says curiously, "Why would someone take a picture of meat and potatoes?" I looked over his shoulder at the photo he was inquiring about. It was not meat and potatoes. It was a toilet bowl; the meat was shit, and the potatoes were toilet paper. My brother had a habit of taking photos of his "more impressive" shits. A photo lasts forever. —MS

Read this page if stoned.

Flounder Flounder Flounder Flounder Flounder Flounder
Flounder Flounder Flounder Flounder Flounder Flounder
Flounder Flounder Flounder Flounder Flounder Flounder
Flounder Flounder Flounder Flounder Flounder Flounder
Flounder Flounder Flounder Flounder Flounder Flounder
Flounder Flounder Flounder Flounder Flounder Flounder
Flounder Flounder Flounder Flounder Flounder Flounder
Flounder Flounder Flounder Flounder Flounder Flounder
Flounder Flounder Flounder Flounder Flounder Flounder
Flounder Flounder Flounder Flounder Flounder Flounder
Flounder Flounder Flounder Flounder Flounder Flounder
Flounder Flounder Flounder Flounder Flounder Flounder
Flounder Flounder Flounder Flounder Flounder Flounder
Flounder Flounder Flounder Flounder Flounder Flounder
Flounder Flounder Flounder Flounder Flounder Flounder
Flounder Flounder Flounder Flounder Flounder Flounder
Flounder Flounder Flounder Flounder Flounder Flounder
Flounder Flounder Flounder Flounder Flounder Flounder
Flounder Flounder Flounder Flounder Flounder Flounder
Flounder Flounder Flounder Flounder Flounder Flounder
Flounder Flounder Flounder Flounder Flounder Flounder
Flounder Flounder Flounder Flounder Flounder Flounder
Flounder Flounder Flounder Flounder Flounder Flounder
Flounder Flounder Flounder Flounder Flounder Flounder
Flounder Flounder Flounder Flounder Flounder Flounder
Flounder Flounder Flounder Flounder Flounder Flounder
Flounder Flounder Flounder Flounder Flounder Flounder
Flounder Flounder Flounder Flounder Flounder Flounder
Flounder Flounder Flounder Flounder Flounder Flounder
Flounder Flounder Flounder Flounder Flounder Flounder
Flounder Flounder Flounder Flounder Flounder Flounder
Flounder Flounder Flounder Flounder Flounder Flounder
Flounder Flounder Flounder Flounder Flounder Flounder

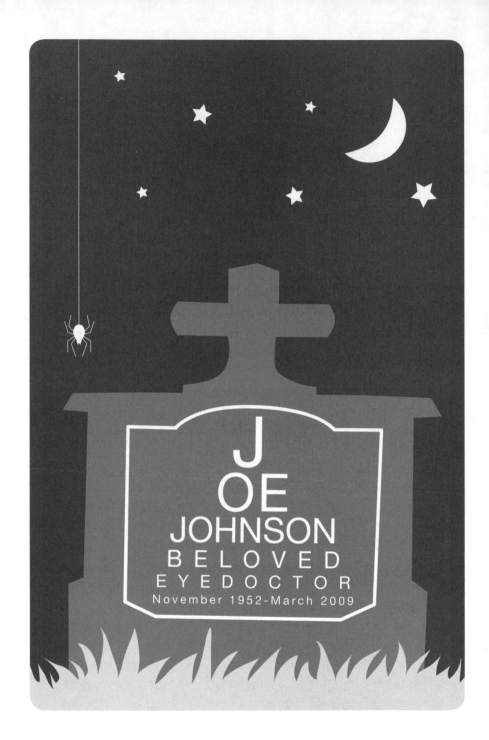

Facts That Sound For a Second Like They Might Be True But Aren't

The Dewey decimal system was originally conceived as a way of organizing pornography.

The reason Dr. Phil grew his mustache is because it helps with his allergies.

Legos were originally created by the military during the Cold War.

A wasp and a sparrow have produced offspring.

The Nazis invented the comma.

Eskimos have 16 words for redundant.

Nostradamus predicted the demise of Grand Funk Railroad.

There is a tribe in Australia who consumes all its food in gaseous form.

A study found that the image found to lower blood pressure the most is a clown sitting on a watermelon.

People in Belgium write diagonally.

Due to a recessive gene, some people become less tan in tanning beds.

Shrimp are actually mammals.

Oliver Wendell Holmes was conceived via anal sex.

WHEN THE BALL DROPS
Great Stories in Diarrhea

at the moment of reckoning,

when there is no tomorrow or yesterday,

when the cork comes out of the bottle...

...the ball drops.

⚠ The Businessman ⚠

I was fresh out of college and on my way to my first job interview. I walked into the lobby of a large, downtown office building, found the floor I needed on a building map, and headed for the escalators. Just before I climbed on, a man approached me from behind. I turned and saw a well-dressed businessman with wild eyes and a sweaty face. "You have to help me," the man told me, "I need a bathroom."

I didn't know what to do. The businessman was clearly in distress, but I was in no position to help. I couldn't very well show up to his job interview with a sweaty stranger tagging along requesting a bathroom key. That wouldn't look good. "I'm sorry, I don't work here."

"I don't care!" the man blurted out, "Wherever you're going, they've got to have a bathroom. Just help me, man!"

I looked the businessman up and down once more, shrugged, and apologized. Turning away from him, I stepped onto the escalator and started my ascent to the mezzanine. A gut-wrenching cry rang out from below and I turned to look back down below. As I slowly craned up and away, I saw the businessman with his pants around his ankles and his arms raised to the heavens. "It's happen-inggggggggg!!!" he cried, as he dropped to his knees and let nature take its course.

—AH

The World's Worst... Museum Exhibits

The Guggenheim's "Create Your Own Jackson Pollack/ Porta Potty"

The Pro Bowling Hall of Fame's "Stick Your Finger in Pro Bowler's Balls"

The Mona Lisa Bonet

The Louvre's Exhausted Foreigners on Benches "Sculpture"

The Museum of Natural History Presents George Washington Carver's Peanut Shoes

The National Zoo's "Feel What It's Like to Be Born Out of an Elephant"

The National Gallery of Art's Audio Tape Guide That Just Says "I Could Do That" at Every Painting

The Hirshhorn's Tammy Faye Baker's Face Pushed Against a Canvas 500 Times

The Museum of American History's "Jean Shorts: An Evolution"

The Air and Space Museum's Turbulence Simulation Urinals

TOILET TRIVIA

Many say that the father of the modern toilet is a British plumber named Thomas Crapper. He perfected the tank that holds the water for flushing, called a cistern. Legend has it that when American soldiers came back from WWI, they used Crapper's name as a euphemism for the toilet.

If E.E. Cummings Wrote
a Poem for This Book

Doo
(d)
O
 o
D[o] o
die
KRAP[s]
Bro   wn
D u t y
in
        tH   e
bo[WL]

Unlikely Novelizations

Girls Gone Wild: The Novel

She pried off the water-saturated mini-T-shirt, the last obstinate cling releasing like the inhibition she was shedding.

"Whoooo-hooooo-yeahhhh" bellowed the crowd who below her awaited their daily feeding of lascivious images like seals at Sea World.

"Whooo-hoo, yeahhhhhh!" confirmed a posse of drunken members of the Kappa Sig fraternity who teetered on a balcony across the street.

Spurred by the wanton courage of her compatriot, the young lady's peer delicately lifted her shirt, exposing part of one breast, as if she were grinning wryly, and then quickly let the shirt recede to gravity's will.

"Seniors '05!" proffered a young man with vomit crusted on the corner of his mouth.

"Whoooo-Yeahhhhhhhhh!" his friend added.

365 Words That Almost Rhyme With Milk

"Kiln," "pill," "chalk." You won't believe how many words almost rhyme with milk!

365 Inside Jokes

This compendium of random people's inside jokes and private references is sure to go over your head, a clear sign of literary merit. Sample Excerpt: "Betty Winnick looks like a paladin!"

365 Dates Of The Year (Not Necessarily In Order)

365 German Words for Suffering

Includes *fendelschmidt*—the pleasure one receives when an actor loses an award and their reaction is caught on film, *eidelfarb*—the fascination experienced upon seeing a dead animal, and *lorfi*—the pleasure had when a camera captures an opposing team's athlete crying because of a loss.

Rejected Smurfs or The Worst Things To Put In Front Of Your Name If You're A Boxer

Festering

Taciturn

Self-aware

Adhesive

Bulimic

Mongoloid

Amorphous

Narcoleptic

Bipolar

★ The Dreamer's Dictionary ☾

Dream Image:		What it Means:
Violin	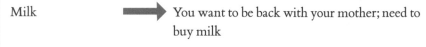	You're gay
Ducks		You want to have sex with a duck
Milk		You want to be back with your mother; need to buy milk
Lorne Michaels		You want to be famous
Lorne Green		You were thinking of Lorne Michaels
Sarah Jessica Parker		You want to have sex with Dee Snyder
On Set of *227*		You are worried about a test
Worried about test		You want to be on the set of *227*; gay
Sand		You want to have sex with sand
Water	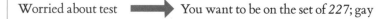	You just peed yourself
Teapots		You are going to die
River		You are repressing a memory of being groped by a Radio Shack employee

TOILET TRIVIA

According to at least one musicologist, most toilets flush in the key of E flat.

The Rabbi

How could this have happened? That was the consensus at the Temple. For years Rabbi Musselman had been a revered member of the community. First, it was overlooked. But alas something was definitely wrong. This was the 8th week in a row that the Rabbi had insisted on giving the service without wearing any pants.

The World's Worst... Colognes

New Tennis Ball

New Jersey Net

Visible

Sour Cream and Chives

Wet German Shepherd

Eau de' Mulch

Unscented

Chunky

Is That Spoiled?

Fleur de' Mokeski

Pretention by Alex Trebec

 # THIS *OR* THAT?

Greek Letter or Friend of my Grandma's at Leisure World?

a. Ada

b. Theta

c. Ida

d. Rita

e. Beta

(Answer: b and e are Greek letters.)

Vocabulary
Builder

Brought to you by Classless Education, making learning bearable since 2007

Yo momma possesses such **largesse**, she'd give me the hair off her back.

lar·gesse (lar JESS)

n. Generosity in gift-giving

Someone who displays largesse is always giving stuff to people or to causes. (It can also be spelled without the last "e," good news if your hand gets tired toward the end of the word.) Although it doesn't have to be used this way, there's often an implied degree of showiness handcuffed to largesse, something Trumpian and showy about the generosity. As in, nobody disputes the value of your gift, buddy, but somehow this gift seems to be more about you than the recipient. Consider the largesse of political lobbyists, who give billions of dollars to political honchos in hopes of cultivating favorable legislation for their many causes. Or take Sean Penn giving his time to help Katrina victims, while his publicist just happened to be around to record his noble largess.

6 Loglines I Pitched in Hollywood That Didn't Sell

1. A dragon is dying of loneliness. A little girl is the only one who believes in him and must try to save him. The dragon later dies and the autopsy reveals it was acute liver failure that killed him. The loneliness was misdiagnosed.

2. What happens when a Spanish conquistador magically travels through time and ends up working at a miniature golf course? Not much.

3. An accountant makes a grave miscalculation. He checks again and corrects the problem avoiding any real distress.

4. A skateboarder is sent back in time to 18th-century England. His body is unable to tolerate and withstand the rigors of time travel and he dies instantly. 2 minutes.

5. A handlebar moustache becomes sentient.

6. A string of extremely violent murders is being conducted by a highly intelligent baked ham.

TOILET TRIVIA

The first paper on a roll was produced by Scott Paper Company in 1890. They did not include their name on the package out of embarrassment.

☞ Ways to Make Things More Exciting...
⚾ **Baseball** ⚾

Cover the outfield wall with 6-inch spikes.

Light the bases on fire.

First base coach replaced with prop comic; if player on first laughs, he is out.

Infield dirt replaced with 2-inch deep tar.

Pitching mound moved to three feet from home plate.

If pitchers balk, they are summarily executed in front of the crowd.

Allow kickball-style "pegging."

7th Inning Stretch followed by 8th Inning Confession.

Populate the outfield with grazing livestock.

Have the warning track heavily trafficked with cars.

If a player hits a ground rule double, the opposing team must renounce their religion.

On deck batter must perform karaoke song of crowd's choice.

Batter stands on dunk tank contraption.

Bullpen is a redneck bar.

9 Failing Thesis Papers

1. Frisbee and Martin Van Buren: Two Things That Have Nothing to Do with Each Other

2. Lincoln and Washington: Who Would Win a Game of One-on-One?

3. Superman Could Too Fly: An Argumentative Essay

4. Do Colored M&M's Taste Different?

5. Just Save Your Time and Give Me the B-

6. How Many Sticks of Chalk Can You Swallow Before Feeling Sick

7. Mary Ann: Actually the Hot One

8. The Wisdom of the Vancouver Canucks

9. A Critique of the About the Author Section of *Crime and Punishment*

Increasingly Egregious Misspellings of Hanukkah

Hannukah

Chanukaha

Ghananka

Chunkyka

Honkeykah

Donkeykong

The World's Worst... Podcasts/Audio Downloads

Flavor Flav Presents The Digits Of Pi

Shoehorn Lore

Best of Emergency Broadcast System Tests

The Wisdom of Q-Bert

Guess The Brand Of Leaf-Blower!

Marcel Marceau's Greatest Hits

Two Hours of Bickering Vietnamese Bureaucrats

"I Got Rim" and Other Poems from Moses Malone

Tony Danza and The Western World: The Oxford Lectures

The Torah as Read By The Guy From Police Academy Who Made All The Crazy Sounds

Thesaurus Excerpts Read in a Thick Indecipherable Scottish Accent

 TOILET TRIVIA

Contrary to what you might think, in a public restroom, the nearest stall to the outside door is the one least likely to be used.

Words That Didn't Make It Into The Dictionary

deodritus
The last remaining flakes of deodorant that you were barely able to scrape off onto your armpit

pleln
The area between your arm and front yard

sampleton
The person in the picture that comes with a wallet

fruttle
Clown feces

crench
When you lean up against the sink and get your crotch wet

chorkan
The act of leaving Reston, Virginia; I *chorkanned* and then drove up I-95

ploof
To lose a contact lens in a urinal

fulcrubacle
When the fat kid ruins seesaw fun

dwoop
To fornicate with a penguin, the act of fornicating with a penguin, (slang) to put on a tuxedo

sornitate
To discuss the war of 1812 with C. Thomas Howell as in "I sornitated at the party and then got some punch," said Roger, as he put his pants back on.

Pornification

Disney Edition

Can you "pornify" the titles below?

101 Dalmatians!

Robin Hood

Aladdin

Sleeping Beauty

The Jungle Book

Monsters, Inc.

The Fox and the Hound

Pocahontas

(Answers on page 40)

---

9 Things To Give Kids on Halloween to Confuse Them

1. Miniature alcohol bottles like they have on airplanes

2. Lamb chops

3. Autographed photographs of Federal Reserve Chairman Ben Bernanke

4. A ladleful of gravy

5. A deed to a fictional ranch

6. Silks and spices the likes of which they've never seen (speak like a pirate)

7. Shaving scum

8. Loose glue

9. Spalding Gray monologue tapes

Pornification

(Answer Key for the quiz on page 39)

101 Dalmatians! = 101 All-Asians!

Robin Hood = Throbbin' Wood

Aladdin = A Lad In

Sleeping Beauty = Seeping Booty

The Jungle Book = The Bung-hole Book

Monsters, Inc. = Monster Stink

The Fox and the Hound = The Foxxe and Her Mound

Pocahontas = Poke-a-hot-ass

The World's Worst... Ice Cream Flavors

Salmon Chunk

Bubble Gum (with already chewed wads)

Ku Klux Kreme

Newsprint

Broccoli Sorbet

Post Nasal Drip Swirl

Roadkill Fudge

Gin

Neapolitan 2: Vanilla, Chocolate, Lint

WHEN THE BALL DROPS
Great Stories in Diarrhea

at the moment of reckoning,
when there is no tomorrow or yesterday,
when the cork comes out of the bottle...
...the ball drops.

⚠ Water Foul ⚠

I always wondered: does shit float? I'm not talking about floating in terms of bobbing up and down in the regular toilet bowl. I wanted to know if it would rise to the surface of a vast fresh water lake.

It turns out the answer is yes. After having spent the afternoon sunning on the deck of my best friend's boat and downing one too many beers, a sudden urge came upon me. It was the unmistakable fecal feeling deep in my bowels and it was not to be ignored.

Miles from shore and under the influence of cheap brew, my only outlet was to jump in the lake and push. All I had to do was pull my bikini to the side and go. It wasn't as easy as it sounds—I had nothing to bear my bottom down and my friends were in the water around me, heckling my attempts to crap. Yes that's right, I decided to crap in the same water that my friends were happily floating in... I had no choice.

Finally with one massive cheek-flapping effort I released a log of doodie that could be mistaken for driftwood by other boaters passing by. The log gently broke the surface of the lake, divided into many pieces and surrounded me like a halo... indeed, I felt like I was in heaven. —AF

Immoral Dilemmas

Are you as ethical as you think?
Read the question below and see how you deal with a difficult moral dilemma.

It's 4am and you are stopped at a red light on a country road that seems like it's never going to change. No one is in sight. Do you masturbate with your left or right hand?

Your father is having an affair and your mother is unaware of it. High five or fist bump?

You hear a woman screaming as if being attacked in the parking lot behind your apartment building. Do you watch *The Office* or *CSI*?

You remarry and find that your new spouse is allergic to the dog you've had for eight years. Who do you put down first?

It's Thursday, and you are raping an antelope. Do you wear a Nixon mask?

You're in your hometown and you bump into your old girlfriend. With your penis. Over and over. Such is life.

 TOILET TRIVIA

In an average year, there are over 40,000 toilet related accidents in the United States.

6 Grant Proposals Turned Down By The Government

1. Arby's Combo Deals: Are They Really A Deal?

2. An Effort to Breed Pigs To Have Mustard And Ketchup In Their Blood

3. Genetic Manipulation to Have the Daily Paper Appear on Human Beings' Skin Each Morning

4. Cocoa Puffs Bird Cereal Addiction Treatment

5. The Jeopardy Theme As It Relates To Mental Processing

6. Correlation Verse Causality Of Shirtlessness And Crime

Unlikely Novelizations

Doom: The Novel

He turned. He shot. The guy died. He turned again. He shot. Another guy died. He turned slightly. He shot. A guy died. He shot again. A guy died. He turned. He shot. He missed. He shot again. A guy died. He turned. He shot. A guy died. He was shot. He lost a portion of his life force. He shot. A guy died. He shot. A guy died. He moved forward. He turned. He shot. A guy died.

 TOILET TRIVIA

On one of her tours back in the day, Diana Ross insisted on having her toilet seats wrapped in cellophane.

Ways to Make Things More Exciting...
Basketball

4 second shot clock.

3 feet tall maximum player height.

Referees selected from pool of Liberace impersonators.

Assistant coaches must be of the genus parrot.

If shot clock goes off, oxygen is removed from arena.

One white guy must touch the ball per every possession.

Game played at 80 degree angle.

There are 50 balls, but only one ball is the "real" ball as declared by a small speck.

No three second violation, but the key is on fire.

Mandatory male perms.

Dozens of pigeons perched on backboard and rim, players awarded three points for killing birds.

 TOILET TRIVIA

There are 35 bathrooms in the White House.

Aphorisms Left Out of Chicken Soup for the Soul

It takes ten years to make an overnight failure.

Success is failure turned inside out (by someone substantially smarter than you.)

There's no "I" in team, though you can get "me." And if you unscramble it, you can spell "meat."

He who seeks only money is the poorest of all, in a vague, insignificant way.

I've found a little remedy to ease the life we live and make each day a happier one: it is the word "vengeance."

When you assume, you make "an assu" out of me.

Actions speak louder than words and accordingly take much more time and effort which are not pleasing to expend.

Laughter is the best medicine for Christian Scientists.

TOILET TRIVIA

The reason that people shake hands with the right hand instead of the left is that in some cultures the left hand was used for wiping after going to the bathroom.

WHEN THE BALL DROPS
Great Stories in Diarrhea

at the moment of reckoning,

when there is no tomorrow or yesterday,

when the cork comes out of the bottle...

...the ball drops.

⚠ WORLD WAR P.U. ⚠

I'm Jewish so I tell this story with great pride. In Amsterdam, there are a lot of ways to have fun but nobody ever talks about what you're supposed to eat between all the fun times you're having.

The last time I was there I ended up at the food stand run by a nice man selling what looked to be delicious sandwiches. Little did I know, the deliciousness would come with a price. I enjoyed one and got on the train to Prague. A few hours later, we stopped for a layover in the German city of Regensburg. I realized I had to go really badly.

Sadly, shitting in Europe is not free, and while I was willing to pay for the privilege, I did not have the right currency (yes, this was in the Pre-Euro era). I ventured out and found a McDonald's but it was closed. Then I found a park with a giant evergreen tree in the corner. I stooped under it like a humiliated dog.

For a second, I couldn't make myself go in public. But I closed my eyes and just tried to imagine myself dropping bombs on Germany circa World War II. And in a few minutes, I had won the war. Too bad I had forgotten the toilet paper. —JM

What Would Jesus Do?

— Basketball edition —

You're down two points with one shot on the line. You missed the first.

WWJD?

Answer: Jesus would not shoot the second free throw, but instead call all players and fans onto the court and arrange a group prayer in gratitude to God.

You threw the ball in bounds but your teammate doesn't see it. As the ball is rolling out of bounds, you think you might be able to call timeout and retain possession.

WWJD?

Answer: Jesus would disregard play and call all players and fans onto the court and arrange a group prayer in gratitude to God.

 TOILET TRIVIA

The first film to show a toilet was *Psycho*. The first TV show to show a toilet was *Leave It To Beaver*.

MEDIUM BITS

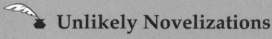

Unlikely Novelizations

Donkey Kong: The Novel

He leaped with all his might over the rolling barrel, fighting to keep his eyes forward and not lift his gaze toward the captive damsel. The hammer hovering mere inches away, it was time to turn the tables. With a last vestige of energy, Mario grasped for the hammer and seized it with the determination of a plumber who had a problem to fix.

"Oh, if my brother Luigi could see me now," thought the mustachioed stereotype. BAM! The barrel was no match for the mighty swing of the stout and proud Italian. BAM! Another barrel was lost to the ether. Onward, Mario trod, the slight incline of the steel girder feeling like the slope of the mighty Everest.

And then he heard it. Whether it was the roar of a rolling barrel or the growl of the giant ape, Mario did not know. What he had no doubts about whatsoever was that the sound shook him to his very core.

→ THIS OR THAT? ←

Pepperidge Farm Cookie or Star of TV's "Who's The Boss?"

a. Danza
b. Verona
c. Light
d. Montieri
e. Milano

(*Answer: b and d are cookies; e, of course, is both.*)

Vocabulary
Builder

Brought to you by Classless Education, making learning bearable since 2007

Yo momma is the **apotheosis** of ugliness!

> **ap·o·the·o·sis**
> (uh poth ee OH sis or ap uh THEE uh ses)

n. The elevation of a person to godlike status; an ideal example

Apotheosis comes from a Greek word that means "to deify," or "to make a god," and it can take that meaning in English: "People credit the teen universe's apotheosis of Britney Spears to a generation-wide tone-deafness." It's more commonly used to mean an ideal example: "The average contestant on *The Apprentice* is the apotheosis of obsequiousness, hoping to kiss his way up Trump's corporate ladder."

A similar word to apotheosis is epitome. Note the pronunciation (i PIT uh mee). We could say that yo mama is the epitome of ugliness. An epitome is a perfect representation of a whole class, type, or idea. If we looked up "ugly" in the dictionary, there wouldn't be a picture of yo momma, but only because it's too ugly to print. We could also say yo momma is the quintessence of ugliness, which means she is the "pure essence" of ugliness.

Product Placement

The growing popularity of TIVO and other digital video recorders (which allow viewers to eliminate commercials) is causing advertisers and networks to create a new concept of television advertising, weaving more product placement into the storylines of popular television shows. Below is a sneak peek at an upcoming episode of *Law and Order*.

EXT. NEW YORK STREET—DAY

Detectives LUPO and BERNARD walk down the street. They examine a dead body in front of them. The dead body wears a jacket that clearly reads Nike, along with Nike shoes.

BERNARD

He sure loved his Nike.

LUPO

Question is "who just did it?"

LUPO takes out a Baby Ruth and takes a bite.

BERNARD

Thought you were on a diet.

LUPO

Baby Ruth has less fat than most candy bars...
Call forensics, let's see what they can turn up.

Close on LUPO taking a big bite of his Baby Ruth.

INT. FORENSICS LAB—DAY

LUPO and BERNARD talk to the FORENSICS TECHNICIAN.

TECHNICIAN

(holding a knife) We found something interesting.

LUPO

(looking at it) Sharp.

TECHNICIAN

Cutco knives never lose their edge.

BERNARD

No pun intended.

TECHNICIAN

Cut right through bone and muscle.

LUPO

Impressive.

Another LAB TECHNICIAN enters. He wears a FUBU jumpsuit, eats from a box of Apple Jacks, and listens to an iPod.

TECHNICIAN 2

(singing) Doo-Doo Doo Doo Doo Doo TJ Maxx!

WHEN THE BALL DROPS
Great Stories in Diarrhea

at the moment of reckoning,

when there is no tomorrow or yesterday,

when the cork comes out of the bottle...

...the ball drops.

⚠ **Poop Tent** ⚠

I went to sleepaway camp for the first time at age 12. That might seem like a late start to camp veterans but I was a mama's girl and did not want to be separated from my family. My first day there was totally nerve wracking—I was five hours away from home and among strangers who all knew each other. These factors all set the stage for a big dump.

My stomach was in knots and I had to go reallllllly badly so I snuck away from my bunkmates to the bathroom, which was three feet away from our beds. Bathroom is a term I use loosely since this was camp and the stalls smelled like old pee and were crawling with spiders.

Scared to sit on an unfamiliar and dirty seat, I squatted, pushed and felt a large log slide out. When I turned around to flush I was shocked that the massive doodie did not land in the bowl but on the back of the toilet just behind the rim. You might think any normal person would grab a piece of toilet paper and nudge the shit into the bowl. But I was not normal. I was 12 and away from home for the first time. Scared shitless (literally), I ran. I left the log of crap just sitting there as if to announce my arrival to the rest of the camp.

Later that day, a bunk meeting was called to bring to the attention of all campers that a large piece of feces was found festering on a toilet bowl just feet from where we all sleep. The camp director announced that this behavior was unacceptable and asked the perpetrator to come forward. I, of course, bonded with my new bunkmates by declaring the mystery shitter a deranged and dangerous person. I never did come forward. And I never did tell anyone the story—not even my husband. Finally, at age 31, I felt compelled to tell my sister the tale. Unloading on her felt just as good and brought just was much relief as the one that inspired this tale in the first place. —AF

The World's Worst... Blues Songs

"I Didn't Get into Harvard (But I Did Get into Brown, my Safety School)"

"Tough To Get Laid in a Name Tag"

"What Is with This Airplane Food, Anyway?"

"Grass Stains Ain't Coming Out"

"Cold Side Is Hot, Hot Side Is Cold"

"Daddy's Dating a Drifter"

"Drowning My Sorrows in Zima"

"Jesus Made Me Fumble"

"Me Beret Is Askew"

"My Papillary Conjunctivitis Is Recurring (It Just Don't Go Away)"

"I Can't Find the Affi-komen (No Matter How Hard I Look)"

Would you rather...

FIGHT TO THE DEATH...
15 GEESE

100 PILLSBURY DOUGH BOYS?

HAVE PHONE SEX WITH YODA

"RAVAGE YOU, I WILL..."

"I WANT YOU TO TOUCH MY BOOBIE AND MY TOOSHY"

SOMEONE WHO HAS A SEXY VOICE BUT USES CHILDISH SEXUAL TERMS?

www.wouldyourather.com

Would you rather...

URINATE THROUGH YOUR NOSE

SMELL THINGS WITH YOUR GENITALIA?

BE ABLE TO MAKE CHANGE FOR A DOLLAR BY PUTTING IT IN YOUR MOUTH

BE ABLE TO MAKE AMISH PEOPLE BREAKDANCE?

www.wouldyourather.com

Bad Board Game Ideas

Rotisserie League Basketball Sets—White Edition

Players choose exclusively white players from the NBA and score points for picks set, hustle baskets, scrapping for loose balls, "doing the intangibles," smart, heady play, unselfishness, moving well without the ball, etc.

Magnetic Militant Black Poetry

The latest expansion set to the wildly successful magnetic poetry, MMBP boasts magnetic tabs on which you'll find words like, "whitey," "die," "the Man," and "oppression." Sample poem: "the Man burns. Whitey Oppression." 300 magnetic tabs in all.

Cop Or Gay?

Take a look at these mustachioed men and tell us? Is he a cop? Or is he gay? 500 Face Cards.

Operation 2000: Cosmetic Surgery Version

"Suck out that fat for 500 dollars." It takes a steady hand to tuck that tummy, hide those crow's feet and inflate those breasts.

How to Host a Mass Suicide

From the makers of *How to Host a Murder Mystery* and *How to Host a Scavenger Hunt* comes this once-in-a-lifetime event. Choose from a number of maniacal, delusional rant-sermons to usher in the great sacrifice to the overlord. Then, select your weapon of choice: group noose, handguns, poisonous elixir, and have a ball! (matching sneakers not included)

Dyslexic Boggle

Anything Counts!

Beat the Shabbos!

You're an Orthodox Jew caught in a traffic jam on Friday afternoon! You need to get home before the sun sets or you'll be violating Judaic law by riding in a motor vehicle during Shabbos. Confront car-jackers, cops, Unitarians, and more in this action-packed role-playing game... So step on the gas, but don't get stuck in gefilte swamp!

Name That Hair

Players guess the origin of different hairs from different parts of bodies/ people/origins (Hair sources range from emu to Gene Shalit's afro).

The Mystery Game

A box, a pad of paper, a pencil, and a bottle of gin. Have fun. $45.00

Actuary! A Role-Playing Game

TOILET TRIVIA

The first production of toilet paper was ordered for a Chinese emperor in 1391.

How Would Seuss Say It

"I'm allergic to clams"

What it would do, I can't truly say

It might make my head spin and spray a green spray

Or cause me to shrink or grow or go gay

Like the curious men in Northern L.A.

Or it might make me sneeze

Or might make me wheeze

I could break out in hives

In the shape of my keys

So no clams for me,

Please.

Please.

Please!

TOILET TRIVIA

The average person uses 57 sheets of toilet paper a day.

Toilet Invention Idea:

"The Toilet Blender"

No more clogs with this "garbage disposal for your toilet."
With The Inshiterator you can stop clogs before they happen.
Just flick the switch and blend away. We chew our food
before we swallow it, right? It's a no-brainer.

4 Bad Names for Boy Bands

1. Ch'Ching
2. Stunted Growth
3. Absolute 0
4. Market Driven

 TOILET TRIVIA

Battle of the Sexes Edition

Most men fold their toilet paper whereas most
women prefer to wad it.

The first event with separate toilets for women and
men was a ball in Paris in 1739.

On average, women spend three times as much
time on the toilet as men do.

WHEN THE BALL DROPS
Great Stories in Diarrhea

at the moment of reckoning,

when there is no tomorrow or yesterday,

when the cork comes out of the bottle...

...the ball drops.

⚠ What I Learned On My Summer Vacation ⚠

I was 16 years old and had just come back from a church trip to Mexico, which was an amazing experience. With all the volunteer work we were doing, there wasn't much time to sleep and I drank coffee for the first time. By the time we got back, I was addicted and totally sleep deprived.

The following Sunday I was to give a speech to my congregation about how the experience in Mexico had opened my heart. I was nervous the night before and didn't sleep well. That morning I had five cups of coffee and felt fantastic. I put on my new, light green, clingy Sunday dress for the occasion.

My presentation went well and after, a lot of people had questions for me—they were interested in having heart opening experiences through charity work as well. I stood at the podium and listened to their questions. Then I felt an unusual ripple in my intestines. As I tried to respond, the ripple got worse and I realized I was in desperate need of a bathroom.

I thought I had enough time to make it home so I excused myself and got in my parents' Army green late '70s Volvo. The ride home was like a scene in a movie. My foot didn't leave the accelerator as I bobbed and weaved through cars and made it home. Phew, I thought. I actually might make this.

I rushed out of the car and got as far as the porch before it happened. I let loose what I hoped was a fart. It wasn't. I took another step to the door and it happened again. I could feel that I had filled my panties with shit.

In the end, what did I learn from my Mexico experience? Sure, it's true that charity work might open your heart, but it's also true that too much coffee will open your anus. —KD

MindF*cks:
8 Things to do in Chruch

1. As people start to solemnly mumble the Lord's Prayer, instead, using the same inflection, recite the lyrics to the 1985 Chicago Bears' "The Super Bowl Shuffle."

2. Replace "Amen's" with "Yeah Boyeeee!'"s.

3. Two words: beach ball.

4. During a Bible lesson, turn to a neighbor and ask, "Where are we, exactly?" Then hold out your book: *Yes I Can, the Story of Sammy Davis, Jr.*

5. Sneeze. When someone says "Bless you," explain that it wasn't you, but rather "Jesus working through you."

6. Ask the person sitting next to you, "Who would win in a fight: Jesus or Zeus?"

7. Claim you are the second coming of the messiah, then perform second rate magic tricks to prove it.

8. Pretend to be drunk at the confession booth; tell priest, "I love you, Dude. . .You're like one of my only real friends, you know? Who needs those sluts anyway, right? Bros before ho's. . .Seriously, I love you like a brother."

Curriculum Vitae for Garnish Man

Objective	To seek an entry level employment at the Hall of Justice
Skills and Powers	Telekinetic powers pertaining exclusively to parsley, ability to read people's thoughts providing they relate to garnish; ability to summon kale; attention to detail
Outfit	Parsley in place of hair, green tights, "GM" on chest and crotch
Experience	· Canadian Hero's League (CHL), 1995-1997, intern · Fought off mutants with dried apple and orange peel · Tricked Mxyzptlk to say his name backwards and go back to the 6th dimension, by saying, "I bet you can't say your name backwards" · Alter ego (barback/server, Houston's Restaurant) · Assisted night shift bar staff
Interests	· Windsurfing · Smiting · Backpacking
References	· Dr. Tundra, CHL · Bob Thomas, manager Houston's Restaurant, Vancouver, BC

What is with airplane crashes? If the only thing that survives the plane crash is the black box, why don't they build the whole plane of that black box? Is it because the material wouldn't withstand the rigors of flight as well as being too heavy and expensive to use in large scale?

Would somebody please explain to me those signs that say, "No animals allowed except for Seeing Eye Dogs?" Who is this sign for, the many non-sight impaired people accompanying blind people as well as those who were considering bringing an animal on the premises?!

What's with the age gap hiring policy at most movie theaters? Didja ever notice, they never hire anyone between the ages of fifteen...and eighty, you know what I mean? Does it have something to do with the sad way old people are treated in this country, increasingly marginalized into obsolescence by new technology?

Answers for Mystery Quiz

1. Austin

2. 2.5

3. Millard Fillmore, Pia Zadora, fifteen pounds of halibut

4. Raddishbaum

5. Not Applicable

6. "Break My Stride" by Matthew Wilder

7. a) Frank Sinatra b) the pancreas

Rejected *Harper's* Index Submission

Number of words in this sentence: 6

Number of words in the previous sentence: 6

Pi to the number of digits that will fit as a ring tattoo across my upper arm: 3.1457965467589

Percentage of white guys who can pull off the expression "that's tight": 5

Number of factual errors in the bible: 56,347

Rank of quantity represented by the numbers 1 and 2, respectively: 2, 1

Percent of blue beverages in sci-fi shows: 90

Grade at which Harriet Tubman ceases being an important historical figure: 5

Number of "cold-themed" flavored gums in 1986: 1 (Wintergreen)

Number of "cold-themed" flavored gums in 2009: fucking ridiculous

Number of times you cheated off the Asian guy in high school: 12

Come on, really: 19

Number of pounds that if she lost she'd actually be pretty cute: 15

Number of words Eskimos have for snow: 137

Number of words Eskimos have for "superfluous": 0

Bad sexual position: 96

Percentage of women in pornos who like to have a man come on their face: 90

Percentage of women in society who actually like it: 5

Number where you can reach me if you are one of those women: 212-555-4020

I am just going to put a random number after this sentence: 159

Number those dudes owe me in U.S. Dollars: $10,000

I'm gonna punch them in the: balls

Number of seconds you've wasted reading this: 75

Number now: 77

Number now if you're a slow reader: 91

Number of people still reading: 7

 TOILET TRIVIA

A person uses the toilet approximately 2,500 times a year.

Euphemisms for Diarrhea

Agent brown

Anal hot chocolate

Aztec two-step

Brownie batter

Bud mud

Bum gravy

Chocolate splat

Chocolate surprise

Chocolate syrup explosion

Cook some hot fudge

Drippy doo-doo

Hershey squirts

Liquid bummer

Liquid doo

Liquid satin

Liquid shit

Montezuma's revenge

Percolating butt coffee

Piss out of your ass

Piss rusty water out of your ass

Reagan's revenge

Rectal hot chocolate

Rectal soup

Shilshul

Shit a flock of sparrows

Spam

The Schlitz

The squirts

The chunky sputters

The runs

The shits

The trots

Trouser chili

Upside down hot fudge sundae

Next Caller

If you don't have time to form your own, whip out this opinion at the next cocktail party you attend:

Boy Scouts

The Boy Scouts have made their position on homosexuality clear. A 1991 Position Statement states: "We believe that homosexual conduct is inconsistent with the requirement in the Scout Oath that a Scout be morally straight and in the Scout Law that a Scout be clean in word and deed, and that homosexuals do not provide a desirable role model for Scouts." That's right, God forbid any gay people get in the way of the manly Boy Scouts as they bedeck themselves in ascots and earn patches for craftwork to be sewn on their green felt sashes. If you're gonna act gay, accept gays. Next caller.

TOILET TRIVIA

During World War II, the German submarine U-120 was sunk as the result of a toilet malfunction.

WHEN THE BALL DROPS
Great Stories in Diarrhea

at the moment of reckoning,
when there is no tomorrow or yesterday,
when the cork comes out of the bottle...
...the ball drops.

⚠ Ivy League Loaf ⚠

One time, while living in Cambridge, Massachusetts, I took a run through Harvard. I'd had a huge dinner but wasn't feeling out of the ordinary.

For some reason, halfway through the run, I really had to go, but I realized I was nowhere near a public restroom. I remembered where the nearest bar was, and started to run in that direction, through the Harvard campus.

It was spring, just before graduation, so they had the tents set up with all the chairs in them. Desperate to hold on, I tried as hard as I could to control my bowels. But things went from bad to worse, and I realized I wasn't going to make it. I looked all around in search of a secluded spot. It turned out I was in luck. I ducked into one of the tents, squatted between the chairs and laid down a huge patty of the nastiest fecal matter imaginable.

I briefly considered attempting to clean up my mess but the logistics were just impossible. I had no way to get rid of the evidence and nowhere to put it even if I did. So I just got up and left. To this day, I like to imagine some WASP-Y parents coming in, so proud of their kid about to graduate, sitting down, and enjoying my work. —CZ

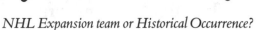

NHL Expansion team or Historical Occurrence?

a. Colorado Avalanche

b. Missouri Compromise

c. Gaston Purchase

d. St. Louis Blues

(Answer: a and d are NHL expansion teams.)

Greek God or Disease?

a. Psoriasis   e. Diabetes

b. Dionysisis   f. Pubic Elves

c. Hermes   g. Hephaestus

d. Herpes   h. The Throb

(Answer: b, c, and g are Greek Gods.)

Smurf or Spice Girl?

a. Brainy

b. Hefty

c. Baby

d. Harmony

e. Scary

f. Vanity

g. Apathetic

h. The Black One

i. Completely and Utterly Retarded

(Answer: a, b, d, and f are Smurfs; c is both.)

Corrections to My Memoir
by Justin Heimberg

Questions have been raised pertaining to the veracity of my memoir, *The Whisper of the Lilac: a Tale of Struggle, Rebirth, and Redemption*. Consequently, I am publishing a few "clarifications" on certain embellishments that I may have included in the book for "effect." Please note, that these tiny little pieces should not taint the overall message of the book.

Corrections:

· I did not kill a man with my bare hands. (P. 67)

· I did not prostitute myself for vegetables in India. (P. 32-38)

· When I said I "killed a leopard," I meant it as a euphemism for masturbation. (P. 2)

· Same with "delivered a baby" (P. 18), "negotiated a gang treaty" (P. 26) and "played Mah Jong with grandma" (P. 124-204)

· I did not write the book. Most of it was dictated to me by a number of day-laborers whom I found at Home Depot. Other parts were cut and pasted from a website about photosynthesis. As for page 43, I don't know where the fuck that came from.

· I did not masturbate a koala for drug money. (P. 81)

· I did it for fun.

· When I said Angelina Jolie was a bad "lay" (P. 204), I meant "actress."

- My "poetry" (Appendices) was taken from Lynyrd Skynyrd lyrics.

- I am not the son of a sharecropper (About the Author). Nor do I have six different sons from seven different mothers. In fact, that is mathematically impossible.

- The font was not Old Goudy Stout. It was New Goudy Stout.

- I did not defeat Jack Johnson for the heavyweight title of the world.

- I never exactly got over that whole crack thing (second part of book).

- I'm high right now.

- The people in the acknowledgements do not exist. I have no friends.

Bad Dances Or Rejected Batman Villains

Pizza Man

Spastic Beaver

The Patrol

The Sprinkler

The Other Kind of Sprinkler

The Doorman

The Lost Contact Lens

The Pie-Eater

MindF*cks:
10 Things to Do in Airports and on Airplanes

In the post 9-11 world, fooling around in airports is a bad idea. Rightfully so, airports are bastions of formality and seriousness. Nonetheless, here are the most hypothetical of all hypothetical airport high jinks. Do not do these or you will subsequently need a list of "funny things to do in Guantanamo."

1. Happily walk toward the metal detector. Scream in agony and convulse as you pass through it. Shoot a fearful look to the person behind you before hurrying off in a glazed shock.

2. Get in a quick work-out by running the opposite way on moving sidewalk. Wear a headband and spandex.

3. Bring individual grocery items including vegetables, deli meat, and hygiene products, and place them on the X-ray conveyor belt. Have your checkbook and supermarket club card out and ready.

4. Wrap a luggage tag around your wrist and ride the baggage carousel motionless.

5. Try to check your luggage: a) one marble b) a horseshoe crab with a red ribbon around it c) an 8" by 10" photo of Konstantin Chernenko.

6. Fill Sudoku grids in the in-flight magazine with the number 6 over and over.

7. At arrival area, hold up a sign that says Zarkon, Galactic Time Traveler of the Year 3000. Wear a silver foil vest and matching arm bands.

8. At metal detector, along with your keys and coins, put the following in trays: a dozen condoms, Mapquest directions to a church, and anal beads.

9. At the carry-on X-ray, instead of a laptop, check a Commodore 64.

10. Report suspicious activity of harmless people, telling security things like, "He only ordered a McGriddle, but there was something about the *way* he ordered it." (We remind you that these are for entertainment purposes. Don't do that.)

Would you rather...

RELAX IN A JACUZZI OF A STRANGER'S SALIVA

OR

HAVE DIARRHEA IN A GRAVITY FREE CHAMBER?

www.wouldyourather.com

TOILET TRIVIA

In Taipei, there is a bathroom themed restaurant, Modern Toilet, where diners eat from plastic toilet bowls and use napkins distributed from toilet rolls.

If Classic Movies Used Product Placement

Ever in search for a dime, movie studios are weighing the idea of re-editing classic films for DVD placing products from advertisers. Here are a few of the changes the studios are considering:

Star Wars: Additional sequence where Luke Skywalker uses the force to make Jiffy Pop popcorn.

Wizard of Oz: Dorothy taps her Nikes together while repeating, "There's no place like Red Lobster. There's no place like Red Lobster..."

Psycho: After a grisly knife stabbing with clearly identifiable Ginsu knife, instead of the notorious shot of blood swirling into shower drain, lingering zoom shot on Pert Plus shampoo.

Snow White: Whole movie is a prolonged NyQuil advertisement; a swig induces Snow White's coma; dwarves' names revised to Sneezy, Achy, Coughing, Stuffy-Head, Fever, and So-You-Can-Rest.

Citizen Kane: Dying words from Kane, not "Rosebud," but rather a cryptic, "I'm going to tempt your tummy with the taste of nuts and honey."

Deliverance: Hillbillies' characters revised to be more sexually responsible so they can plug Trojan brand condoms.

Casablanca: "Here's looking at you kid" followed by a dramatic pause and forlorn swig of YooHoo chocolate drink.

The Ten Commandments: 11th commandment: Thou shall not pay a lot for this muffler.

WHEN THE BALL DROPS
Great Stories in Diarrhea

at the moment of reckoning,
when there is no tomorrow or yesterday,
when the cork comes out of the bottle...
...the ball drops.

⚠ Dog Doodie ⚠

I was on my honeymoon in Hawaii digesting my seafood lunch. My wife and I were driving along a beach road, past bright flowers, palm trees and surfers on their way to catch a wave. It all would have been really romantic—if I didn't need to take a shit.

After a few minutes, beads of sweat were popping up all over my face. If I clenched my anus any more I feared I would suck my body up inside of it. Since I didn't get the "I crapped my pants" insurance on the rental car, my new wife ordered me to pull over to the side of the road and squat in the tropical bushes. Armed with a wet wipe (my brilliant bride always carried them in her purse) I leapt into the brush and pissed out of my ass. A series of wipes later and I was clean, but with no garbage pail in sight. I did the un-environmentally friendly thing and tossed my stained, crapped-up wipes by the side of the road. Relief was upon me but then suddenly I was gripped by fear. I heard a rustling in the bushes. Out of nowhere, a mangy mutt charged up to me, sniffed, grabbed the poop wipe off the ground and happily scampered off. —AF

TOILET TRIVIA

In 2008, the Himeji City Museum of Literature in Japan debuted an entire exhibit devoted to poop.

The World's Worst... Theme Clubs

Under Construction:

In the tradition of fabricated dilapidation comes this intentionally unfinished space that gives patrons the feeling that they have discovered the club early, before it becomes gentrified and trendy. An official Under Construction sign will ward away the uninformed while beckoning the cultural elite to the club that redefines gritty. Once inside, you'll find a half-done hot spot complete with exposed piping and insulation and several tiers of scaffolding/dance floors. The bartenders are dressed like construction workers; one takes forever to take your order while the others stand around and watch. Throughout the night, patrons can collaboratively build projects or continue construction on the club with the various hardware that is available, or witness various functional performance art acts where bands build while they play. You'll have to sign a waiver at the door, as power tools and alcohol can be a dangerous combination. Companion clubs include Under Destruction and Under Deconstruction.

Stoops:

Police line tape replaces velvet ropes at the door to this "little inner city." Askew shutters and pealing paint cover facades of low income homes, in front of which cascade the eponymous stoops for sitting. Beverages are served in brown bags, and while malt liquor forties are the house drink, mixed drinks can be bagged as well. Dance along an asphalt dance floor with potholes and chalk outlines, and partake in graffitiing the walls with complementary spray paint.

Oy Vey:

Following the precedent set by The Limelight, a church turned club, comes the not quite as ornate Oy Vey, a club converted from an old synagogue. Unlike The Limelight, which spoiled its theme by not going all-out (right after-the-fact confession, communion wafer hors d' ourves, water into wine drink specials, sign-of-the-cross dances, etc.), Oy Vey makes the most of its offensive gimmick with dovening on the dance floor, live brisses, and bargain prices.

The Third Grade:

After being ushered in by an orange-sashed patrol/bouncer, "Students" get their groove on in a spacious elementary cafeteria style-dance floor adjacent to a lunch-line style bar where an untraditionally attractive lunch lady serves up drinks in beverage boxes and pouches, while food is served on Styrofoam trays. Friday night is Pizza night, followed by Sloppy Joe Saturday. Food and beverage trading is encouraged and food fights are expected. Guest bands supplement traditional instruments with woodblock, triangle, and recorder. For the wild at heart, the patio combines an outdoor bar with a live dodge ball game.

Club '80s:

The nation's premier retro '80s club: 1880s, that is. Heated by a model of Carnegie's steel furnace, with tracks of magnates' expanding railroads running throughout the club, Club '80s is the perfect antidote to all those redundant cheesy 1980s clubs. Dance to techno/industrial versions of Wagner's "Pasifal", Brahms' Symphony 7, and the best of Gilbert and Sullivan, while perusing the decor, such as the portrait of President Grover Cleveland, the 1885 birth certificate of physicist Neils Bohr, and articles about Robert Koch's method of a preventive inoculation against anthrax. Remember those crazy '80s?!.

Club Waiting Room:

Admission is based on how patient you look. Once inside you sign a clipboard and thumb blindly through *Highlights* and *Reader's Digest*. Cheap mall art hangs on the walls and the "DJ" consists of an office assistant occasionally calling out names from the clipboard. Once your name is called you proceed to another waiting room with no magazines.

Pop Culture Major Syllabus

SOC 235: Grimace: Psychosocial Aspects

Ronald McDonald is a clown. Simple enough. Mayor McCheese is a man with a cheeseburger for a face. Still comprehensible. The Hamburglar is a vaguely humanoid creature, of modest deformity perhaps, but nonetheless, human. But as for Grimace, what the hell is he? An investigation into the nature of Grimace's paradoxical amorphous "non-identity" identity and it's socio-political effects on contemporary western culture, examined in a theoretical frame-work of Chomskian innate language faculty. Students will write one short paper, one longer paper, and construct one diorama.

PSC 360: Governmental/Economic Systems in Smurf Societies

The evolution of Smurf governmental structure from primitive tribalism to full-fledged Marxist communism. Topics include a) The Gargamel/Azrael master-slave dialectic; and b) the pros and cons of the Smurfberry as a unit of currency. Also, who were the gay Smurfs? Students will write one long paper, give one oral presentation, and get one tattoo.

ENG 175: Shampoo Bottle Labels as Literature

A collection of shampoo and conditioner texts central to Western hygiene from antiquity to the modern age, examined from a variety of critical and theoretical standpoints. Texts include Pert, Prell, Finesse, Pantene, Pert Plus, Pert Minus (not quite a shampoo, not quite a conditioner) and excerpts from Head and Shoulders. Topics include moisturizing motifs and the use of Ammonium Lauryl Sulfate as symbolism. Also, what is meant when the authors of Pantene's "Avoid Accidents" chapter tell us "if swallowed, drink a glassful of water to dilute"? Students will write three short papers and keep one "hair journal".

ENG: 320 Shakespeare/ Benny Hill: A Comparative Study

A detailed look at selections and completed works of both bawdy Brits. Emphasis on language and on slapping little bald sidekicks as a means of utilizing dishonor as a sanction. Also, consideration of several new emerging theories, 1) in his original drafts, Shakespeare ended both *Hamlet* and *Macbeth* in typical Hill-esque farce, with his characters frantically chasing half-dressed meter-maids to the accompaniment of bouncy chase music, and 2) that Benny Hill and Shakespeare are actually the same person. Students will write one long essay and one ridiculously long essay.

HST 20: Scott Baio and the Western World

Introduction to Baio's life, works, and criticism, (in the context of television culture in the 1980s) and their effect on western thought. Baio's career from his early days on *Happy Days* to his often forgotten work in *Zapped* to his masterful performance in *Charles in Charge*; with in-depth analysis of Chachi's leg-sash of machismo. Prerequisites: ENG 186: Segues: Post-Seinfeldian; LIT 35: Hasselhoff Lore, and IDC 430 Fabio: Cross-cultural Perspectives.

MTH 220: Differential Geometry in Connect Four

Differential manifolds, fiber bundles, connections, curvature, Riemannian geometry including submanifolds and variations on the length integral, complex manifolds, homogenous spaces, and other "pretty sneaky" strategies. Prerequisites include MTH 56: Special Topics in Stratego Multivariate Statistics and MTH 45: Asymptotic and Perturbation Methods in Battleship.

EXTRA! EXTRA!

Last year DVDs accounted for 70% of Disney's profit. According to surveys, one of the most popular reasons to buy DVDs was because of the "extras"—supplementary features such as extended footage, behind the scenes segments, cast interviews, etc.

Star Wars Trilogy—Deluxe Edition—2 discs of Extras!

Optional voice-over commentary by Chewbacca

40 minutes of additional director's cut footage including:

· Sequence where a young Luke Skywalker uses the force to make Eggs Benedict
· Chewbacca's lengthy shower and shampoo scene
· Yoda's Bar Mitzvah
· Wampa secluded in ice cave, listening to AM talk radio

Speedometer-like tally on bottom of the screen showing the increase in George Lucas' wealth as you watch the movie.

Barbara Walters interview with Greedo, wherein the second-billed bounty hunter cries, confessing a troubled childhood and feelings of inadequacy

Passion of the Christ...

Unseen failed *Passion of the Christ* spin-off sitcom pilot—"Oh Christ!"—What would happen if Jesus didn't die on the cross and married and had children? Ted Danson stars as Jesus, Steven Weber as Judas.

Are you a blaspheming Jew?—Interactive

If you don't have time to form your own, whip out one of these opinions at the next cocktail party you attend:

No More Best Actor and Best Actress Awards.

With Hillary and Palin having made their pushes for the White House, we can now unequivocally conclude that women want an even playing field. They want to compete with the boys in anything and everything. Nobody is demanding there be one female president and one male president. There is no female and male winner for a Pulitzer Prize. There's no "Best Screenwritress Award." So why do we need Best Actress AND Best Actor? Yes, they play different roles, but writers write from different points of view. Some female roles are more similar to male roles than male roles are to each other. There is race equality in acting, but not gender equality. We don't have "Best Black Actor." We'd then need, of course, Best Black Actress, Best Black Actress in a Supporting Role, etc. . Absurd. Next caller.

Make it Legal to Sell Cigarettes to Young People; and Illegal to Sell Them to People over 40

Studies show the long term effect of smoking only has significant ill effects on health when people smoke after 40. If people quit before then, expected lifespan is about one year shorter than that of non-smokers. Not that big a deal. Yes, starting young brings with it the possibility of nicotine addiction, but a 16 year old has 24 years to quit before the health hazards get serious. Plus, they probably won't like it that young which decreases their likelihood of getting hooked. Not to mention the fact that the rebellion is gone if it's something they can do, and their parents can't. Bottom line, every year you smoke after 40, the health risks increase exponentially, wasting US tax dollars on medical costs that could have been avoided if you shifted your smoking ten years earlier. Ban cigarettes sales to the middle aged. Next caller.

WHEN THE BALL DROPS
Great Stories in Diarrhea

at the moment of reckoning,

when there is no tomorrow or yesterday,

when the cork comes out of the bottle...

...the ball drops.

⚠ The Little Leaguer ⚠

I was 9 and quite the baseball fan. The Milwaukee Brewers were (and still are) my team and many of my waking hours were spent reading the box scores from the night before, waiting for that day's game to begin, and—during the main event—throwing a tennis ball against the garage door and listening to Bob Uecker and Patt Hughes call the game on 1310 AM, WIBA Madison.

I was also an avid little-leaguer, and one season I played for the M&I Bank Angels. We wore red, oozing Badger pride, and I found myself catching for the first time, proud to be the only catcher in the league who wasn't the team's fat kid.

At our first practice of the season we were excited to learn that during the off-season the league had put in new bathrooms. Just one step away from the big leagues now...

We were a few innings into a practice game, and after squatting for an hour I quickly became aware that I needed to take care of something, so in full catcher's regalia (which effectively doubled my volume), I trotted up the hill to avail myself of the new facilities. By now, my gastro-needs were trumping my interest in architecture and I quickly reached for the doorknob to let myself in. Locked. This is not good.

They had put up two separate buildings, each quite small, one for girls and one for boys. I thought, luckily, they couldn't possibly lock the girls room too. Forgetting for the time being that there were, of course, no girls in the league, I impending-shit-waddled over to the other side, ready to throw 9-year-old taboos aside, only to encounter a second locked door.

The only option I saw was in an alleyway between the two buildings. For some reason, I used to wear spandex biking shorts underneath my cup and my white baseball pants, so it was a lot of onion layers to peel back and I didn't make it in time. The ball had dropped. It was a fatal internal switch that I just couldn't turn back. I was innocent no more. With no time to think—let alone remove the catcher's chestguard or shin armor—I barely got my pants unbuckled before I was spraying the alleyway.

The park was empty except for our team. There was no one around. They had literally finished construction a day or two before and there were still building materials strewn about—a post-Apocalyptic landscape upon which to paint my Pollock.

My only recourse was to sit there sobbing and completely covered in my own maelstrom until Randy, my babysitter, got to wondering what was taking me so long and came looking for me. I don't remember much after that, like what became of the shit-soaked baseball gear, but he got me home and an hour or so later I was in a bathtub. In retrospect, a shower might have been a better choice. —ABB

TOILET TRIVIA

Common causes of diarrhea include bacterial
infection, allergies, malabsorption, and stress.

Crafty Clarence

As little kids, everyone in the neighborhood tried to dig holes to China. "It can't be done. You're a silly schmuck," scoffed everyone's parents. But nothing could discourage Clarence. He got a shovel and dug, dug, dug. Years later it was uncovered that Clarence had been a German spy. You see, while the foolish people laughed, he had dug trenches for the advancing Blitzkrieg. That is the story of how one little boy helped conquer France.

The World's Worst... Harry Potter Sequels

Harry Potter and the Wonders of Alcohol
A drunken binge results in the destruction of a small Iowa town.

Harry Potter and the Hired Prom Date
The whole school is perplexed when Harry shows up to the dance with a mysterious 24 year old he "met in Canada."

Harry Potter and the Jheri Curl Debacle
An egregious fashion faux pas causes Harry to lose standing among fellow magicians.

Dirty Harry Potter
Sick and tired of feeling like an outcast, Harry takes to the streets, intent on using his powers for evil instead of good.

Harry Potter and the Retarded Penguin
Harry befriends a lonely animal; then, shortly thereafter, abandons it.

Harry Potter and the Chunky Cheerleader
As Harry matures, he realizes that beautiful doesn't always mean easy.

Harry Potter 2: Electric Boogaloo
Turbo and Ozone teach Harry the difference between breakin' and poppin'.

 TOILET TRIVIA

In the 1970s, Johnny Carson joked about a toilet paper shortage on *The Tonight Show*, causing a run on toilet paper across America.

Facts That Sound For a Second Like They Might Be True But Aren't

Abe Lincoln actually pronounced his name "Ah-bay."

The walrus has been known to kill its prey with its penis.

Confederate President Jefferson Davis invented the high five.

There are over 19 fonts banned by the FCC.

Water on the left side of the pool is always colder than water on the right side.

The back of a stamp has 70% of the daily requirement of vitamin C.

Leonardo Da Vinci invented the scissor in the 1500s. It wasn't until 300 years later when the second scissor was added, making "scissors" useful.

Both Hitler and Napoleon were missing a testicle. Weirder still—it was the same testicle. Scientists found it in 1987.

The sound of thunder is not actually caused by lightning strikes. It's just, like, a crazy coincidence.

Eli Whitney had six testicles.

The wheelbarrow was never invented.

For inspiration when composing music, Mozart soaked his left hand in a bowl of wet spinach.

In the time it takes you to read this sentence, 900 trapeze artists will die.

Shaquille O'Neal's father is Chinese.

The average Romanian spends 27 years looking for his keys.

A sloth bite is deadly over a period of 200 years.

The Russian alphabet only has 4 letters.

John Quincy Adams was the world's first bisexual.

Ulysses S. Grant was buried with his trombone.

Tommy Hilfiger's real name is Merle Klendendorf.

George Washington Carver's last words were "Fuck peanuts."

A rhinoceros' taste buds are on its scrotum.

You are born with over 300 bones, but by the time you die, you only have 250.

How Would Seuss Say It

Famous Quotes Edition

"I see dead people"

If I look really closely I see the deceased

Walking around all gross and diseased

Doing whatever it is that they please

I see dead policeman and dead astronauts

And dead certified public accountants a lot

I see Elvis, Buddy Holly, and Stevie Ray Vaughn

Playing Scrabble together on the deck on my lawn

Dead princes and queens and dukes and kings

Dead ringmasters busy as they master their rings

I see all kinds of crazy dead things

Like the dead trumpet sheep from Sacataw Springs

Who play their noses like horns with mournful glee

As more dead people arrive in PurgatoREE

Oh the so many dead people I see!

"He's using fuzzy math."

He adds and divides, he subtracts and timeses

But his numbers are forced like very bad rhymses

$4 + 4 = 6, 9 - 3 = 8$

Think that's bad?

It gets worse

Just you wait

3 times 3 is a hundred and thirty thirteen

No sir, his math, it isn't quite clean

It's gone through some kind of distorting machine

Making thin numbers fat and fat numbers lean

What's making these numbers appear so fuzzy?

He wasn't adding fuzzy dust, was he?

Maybe it started a long time ago

Or maybe it's just this batch of bad blow.

Back to Reality

To: Rupert Murdoch
From: Fox Development
Re: Derive and Conquer Initiative

According to recent Nielsens, current reality programming ratings are dropping. However, since scripted programs are not cost-effective for the network, we have decided to retool, rework, and recombine a number of existing reality shows to see if we can revive interest before having to resort to actually (God forbid) writing. See below for the summer schedule:

Mormon Bachelor...

Tagline: *The Bachelor* with a twist...

Summary: 30 hopeful beautiful single ladies compete, but only 3-5 will be chosen to be the wives of the... *The Mormon Bachelor*. Has all the drama and romance of traditional dating shows, with added elements. For example, consider the intrigue when the Mormon Bachelor finds a girl he really likes but she doesn't get along with the other prospective spouses, threatening the cohesiveness of the unit. Target Demographic: women 25-29, Utah.

The Complex Life

Tagline: A reverse *The Simple Life*

Summary: Alan Greenspan and Steven Hawking go clubbing, indulge in giggly Madison Avenue shopping sprees, and have uncomfortable sex with disreputable partners.

Target Demographic: professional men 29-49 (attractive to advertisers).

The Biggest Luger

Tagline: *The Biggest Loser* meets the *Great American Race*

Summary: Everyone loves to watch a big man in a small sled! It's all about getting down the hill the fastest for the fattest, as these obese men and women bundle up and use their bulk to thunder down a dangerously icy chute. Possible marketing slogans include: Did someone say "Avalanche?" and Hope they don't eat the ice!

Target Demographic: Lovers of Schadenfreude, people who need to feel better about their lives, my friend Larry (he loves this kind of stuff).

Other ideas in incipient stages of development:

My Big Fat Obnoxious Brain Surgeon

Foreign or Retarded? (game show)

The "Women Sit in a Hut Until Their Menstrual Cycles Align" Show

America's Top Model Train

Celebrity Pile-On

Fear Factor Light: Gil Gerard throws racquetballs at you for a couple of minutes

MindF*cks:
4 Things to Do at a Wedding

1. Set up army men scaling the wedding cake.

2. When the official asks if there are any objections, stand up and go into a ten minute diatribe about Vin Diesel's unwarranted movie career success. Swear often.

3. Instead of confetti, throw a) marbles, b) poppers, c) minnows.

4. Swap the audio of the traditional "Here Comes the Bride" with a) "Wipeout," b) *The Dukes of Hazzard* theme, c) Whale mating calls.

WHEN THE BALL DROPS
Great Stories in Diarrhea

at the moment of reckoning,
when there is no tomorrow or yesterday,
when the cork comes out of the bottle...

...the ball drops.

⚠ Backyard Blues 2 ⚠

Our plumbing had been backed up for more than a day, all of it. Though I did not know it at the time, tree roots had grown into the master pipe and caused an obstruction. This caused all our toilets and showers to cease draining, and after a while, sewage began to actually bubble up through our shower drains, creating small geysers of fecal water.

The plumber was coming the next day but I had to go desperately. It was after midnight, so any place around us with a restroom was closed. I debated using a Ziploc bag, but instead decided to go into the backyard to cop a squat. And so I did. The next day the plumber came and explained to us that in order to check the plumbing he'd need to look at the "master valve," something I had never heard of.

"Where is it?" I asked.

"Somewhere in the backyard."

He scouted for the valve entry point, which—you guessed it—happened to be about six inches from my day old crap. When he came back in, I could not help but smirk. I asked if he found everything OK and he looked at me as if his eyes had seen it all, and said, "I thought that was human shit." —JH

Euphemisms for White Basketball Players
(As quoted from real publications)

Lacks natural ability but makes up for it with heart and hustle

Coachable and team oriented, he makes those around him better

Compensates for lack of jumping ability with heady play

Instinctive and bright, understands team's complex system

Hard working rebounder, despite short arms

Excellent rhythm in his catch and pass skills

Capable of hitting the short jumper

He is an aerospace engineering major

Always wears the right sized shoes

Washes his jersey impeccably

Sets awesome picks

Great work ethic

Unselfish player

Works hard in practice

Overachiever

Scrappy

Always fights for loose balls

Proficient at drawing fouls

Plays great defense

Shows up every night

Moves well without the ball

Does all the intangibles

Team oriented banger

Super Villain Resume:
The Male Cheerleader

Objective	To find employment as a super villain in the Legion of Doom
Education	Four years at USC
Moment Turned Evil	After being dropped on head when thrown into the air during group cheer
Villain Experience	Double life at night, hatched numerous plots to cause general chaos in city and to become rich
Motivation	Embittered by age of cynicism and lack of school spirit, secretly jealous of athletes and popular people
Skills and Powers	Able to brainwash large groups of people and individuals to do my bidding with pep; indomitable spirit; acrobatics
Outfit	USC cheerleading garb, megaphone
Special apparatus	Magic megaphone which spews mind-control cheers Horde of mascots at my disposal to do my bidding

♪Pornification♨

For every movie, there exists, at least theoretically, a porno version of that movie. Can you "pornify" the titles below?

Broadway/Musical
The Jazz Singer

Ragtime

Fiddler on the Roof

Oklahoma!

Grease

The Sound of Music

M. Butterfly

Television
Meet the Press

Murphy Brown

NYPD Blue

Everybody Loves Raymond

NUMB3RS

Happy Days Sequels
Mork and Mindy

Joanie Loves Chachi

(Answers on page 98)

Pornification

(Answer Key for the quiz on page 97)

Answers: Broadway/Musical:

The Jazz Singer = The Jizz Slinger

Ragtime = Gagtime

Fiddler on the Roof = Diddler on the Roof

Oklahoma! = Oklahomo!

Grease = Crease

The Sound of Music = The Pound of Pubic

M. Butterfly = M. Butterface

Television:

Meet the Press = Press the Meat

Murphy Brown = Murphy's Brown

NYPD Blue = NYDP Blue

Everybody Loves Raymond = Everybody Loves Rimmin'

NUMB3RS = THUMB3RS

Happy Days Sequels:

Mork and Mindy = Porkin' Mindy

Joanie Loves Chaci = Joanie Loves Bukkake

 TOILET TRIVIA

Only one person in three washes his or her hands when leaving a public restroom.

MindF*cks:
12 Things to Do to Screw with a Driving Test Examiner

1. Straddle the dotted lane-dividing lines on highway. When the examiner asks what you are doing, explain you are "playing Pac-Man."

2. Signal right when you turn left and vice versa. As you exit the car, make sure the examiner sees you have your shoes on the wrong feet.

3. Blast gangsta rap.

4. Blast NPR.

5. Blast imaginary space ships.

6. Unprompted, ask extremely personal questions about the examiner's life like "Have you ever truly been in love?" and "Do you believe in God?"

7. Drive to the beat of the music.

8. Wear uncomfortably revealing jean shorts.

9. As you enter the car, take your key out and act puzzled as to where the key goes. Be unable to solve this problem. After a minute, sigh and say in a resigned voice, "Just not in the cards today, I guess."

10. Put in a "How to Learn German" CD and engage the exercises, practicing loudly and intensely.

11. Start driving on the wrong side of the road and, in an awful British accent, ask how many kilometers per hour you can go.

12. Have two dozen notches cut in your steering wheel along with a pocket knife below the dash. If the examiner asks about the notches, answer without emotion: "Some questions are best left unanswered."

Euphemisms for Fart

Anal salute

Beef

Beep your horn

Blast the chair

Blow the big brown horn

Bottom blast

Bottom burp

Break wind

Butt burp

Butt trumpet

Cut a stinker

Cut the cheese

Drop a bomb

Flatulence

Float an air biscuit

Funky rollers

Gaseous intestinal by-products

HUMrrhoids

Honk

Jet propulsion

Let each little bean be heard

Mating call of the barking spider

One gun salute

Pass gas

Pass wind

Poot

Puff the Magic Dragon

Rebuild the ozone layer

Rectal honk

Rectal shout

Shoot the cannon

Singe the [noun] (e.g. carpet)

Toot

Toot your own horn

Facts That Sound For a Second Like They Might Be True But Aren't

Schlitz Brewery owns half of the Vatican.

A small amount of heroin is used in the manufacturing of SunnyD citrus drink.

Crabs can be taught simple addition.

Isaac Newton discovered gravity when he was making a "number 2."

Soccer was invented on pirate ships as a means of cleaning the deck.

Cheech and Chong borrowed the plots of their movies from Arthur Miller plays. And vice-versa.

The fallopian tube is neither a tube nor fallopian.

Abe Lincoln wore his top hat because he was an amateur magician.

Shakespeare coined the phrase "mofo."

A Koala bear's testicles are transparent.

The most constipated animal in the world is the polar bear.

A typist's fingers will travel 8 million light years in a lifetime.

The Statue of Liberty's real name is Sheila.

Life Savers have holes because they were originally used as fish bait.

Sir Mix-A-Lot is a real knight; however contrary to popular belief, he mixes in moderation.

The kings in a deck of cards represent the members of Bachman Turner Overdrive.

The bagpipe was originally made from human lung.

Car alarms cause more thefts/vandalism than they prevent.

Baboons are the only other species to partake in oral sex.

Martin Luther King invented the fair catch.

The Chinese Government removes "extraneous" organs from their female gymnasts and wrestlers to make then lighter.

3 of the 5 original members of Sha Na Na are now congressmen.

The checkmark was originally a letter in the alphabet.

If a statue in a park of a person on a horse has both front legs in the air, the person died during sex.

WHEN THE BALL DROPS
Great Stories in Diarrhea

at the moment of reckoning,
when there is no tomorrow or yesterday,
when the cork comes out of the bottle...
...the ball drops.

⚠ Curry Up! ⚠

A very sweet coworker, who always seemed to want us to be more than just coworkers, once invited me over to her place for dinner. I accepted the invitation and had no apprehension when told that she would be preparing a home-cooked Bengal curry. The meal was fine—spicy but fine— but about an hour and about three Kingfisher lagers into the evening, I began to feel some minor gastric distress just as we were moving past the dinner portion of the evening. She lived in one of those unique-to-New York City apartments where the bathroom was a former closet with the toilet jammed so tight next to the bathtub that anyone other than Kate Moss would be compelled to dangle a leg into the tub to do any serious business. To make matters worse, the only sink to be found was in the kitchen. Knowing this, and having a sinking feeling of where this was going, I claimed to have suddenly taken ill and told her I really had to go.

I left her scratching her head trying to figure out where she went wrong and headed down to the street. I even managed to snag a cab for the 60-some block ride from her place to mine. For the first twenty blocks, as the cab seemed to hit every red light, I started to worry. For the next twenty blocks, panic set in. For the final twenty blocks, I started looking for businesses that might possibly have a restroom worth leaping out of the cab for. At long, long last, we pulled onto my block, and I began to realize that I was going to go very soon and, from the way things were churning, it wasn't going to be pretty.

I threw a $20 bill at the cabbie and made a beeline for the door of my walk-up. I made it to the third floor landing, just one floor away from relief, when it started. With a gut-blasting fart, my one and only experience with foam-like diarrhea began. My race upstairs slowed to a crawl as I tried in vain to pinch my ass cheeks together to contain the barrage. But there's no holding back destiny. Surrendering to the inevitable, and hoping like hell my roommate wasn't home, I let loose and resumed my sprint to my apartment. Imagine the worst curry smell possible combined with the fetid odor of wet turd and I can assure you it would still smell better than this did. It was a no-win situation for my boxers, and I felt bits hit my legs on their way down as my pants filled.

Thank God my apartment was empty. I stripped and went straight to the shower to clean up. I took my boxers and pants in with me and managed to get them clean enough that I could take them to the laundromat without smelling like a flea market port-o-san.

My roommate arrived as I was getting dressed.

"Hey," he greeted me, "Any idea why there's a line of foul-smelling shit leading straight to our door from the third-floor landing?"

I probably could have owned up to it, but I played dumb. Of course he knew. And of course I knew he knew. But I never admitted it. Until now.
—Boomer

TOILET TRIVIA

In November 2001, the inaugural World Summit on Toilets was held in Singapore.

Standard Download Agreement

This agreement licenses the software and contains warranty information and liability disclaimers. By selecting the "download" button (installing the software), you are confirming your acceptance to the software and agreeing to become bound by the terms of the Agreement.

1. The Licensor grants to you, the Licensee, a nonexclusive right to use the software (hereinafter "the Software") for ninety (90) days in accordance with the terms of this agreement. You may use the Software on one (1) computer.

2. You may not make or distribute copies of the Software, or electronically transfer the Software from one computer to another or over a network. You may not decompile, reverse engineer, disassemble, or otherwise reduce the Software to a human-perceivable form.

3. You may not talk negatively about the Software with any of your friends in any way, whether directly, or through veiled euphemism, or even jerk your head or point in the direction of the Software while making disparaging noises.

4. If you run any computer games using the Software, upon achieving high scores, under no circumstances are you permitted to enter lewd or suggestive three (3) letter combinations such as "S-E-X", "A-S-S", or "T-N-A." You are permitted to, and encouraged to enter "M-R-T."

5. Limitations of Damages- NO WARRANTIES. The company expressly disclaims any warranty for this software. Documentation is provided "as is" without warranty express or implied. The entire risk arising out of use or performance of the Software remains with you. Asshole.

6. Do NOT pass go. Do NOT collect 200 dollars.

7. Registration—We will ask for information that personally identifies you or allows us to "contact" you. If you do not grant us such personal information you will still be allowed to use the Software, though it is significantly more difficult to do so with no fingers... and a grotesquely misshapen testicle.

When you enter your personal information, you automatically grant us a trademark on your name in all major classes and subclasses. Accordingly, you will pay us any time said name is written or spoken, and/or you must change your name to something clearly dissimilar. The Company owns trademarks for all letters other than B, L, and X and all numbers (Arabic, Roman, and Heiroglyph) except the number 8. Common name changes include BLX8, 88XBL, and the sound of a handful of change landing on a table.

8. You no longer have free will.

9. General—This Agreement shall be governed by the internal laws of 12th Century Prussia, wherein cruel and unusual punishment was quite popular.

Failure to adhere to the Agreement and all clauses hereuntowhereinafore will result in immediate organ removal and auction.

10. I rule you—Looks like maybe you shouldn't have picked on the nerdy kid in high school, after all. Kind of regret calling me "dorkwad" and "jerkwad" and other pejoratives with the suffix "wad." Will you go to prom with me now, you little hussy? Look who's got all the power now! I can have you killed with a push of a button. You may already be too late...

I Agree, Download Now ⬇   Cancel ✕

LONG PIECES

Ouch!

Dennis felt a sharp pain stab his right leg. He must have bumped his knee into the corner of the desk. Ow, that smarts! But then Dennis looked down and the pain stopped. You see, Dennis's leg had been amputated a couple months ago and he was just experiencing "phantom limb syndrome." Boy, was he relieved.

The Little Train

"I think I can. I think I can," chugged the choo-choo, and he continued to struggle up the hill. "I think I can. I think I can... although I'm not 100% positive." The little engine slowed down. "Tough to say at this point. Could go either way. But perhaps I can." He slowed some more. "Doesn't look good," he admitted. "Let's not delude ourselves." He began to roll back down the hill. "Shit," said the choo-choo.

MindF*cks:
25 Things to Do at a Supermarket

1. Take the checkout dividing bar and place it on the ground between you and the person behind you as opposed to between your respective grocery items. Shoot aggressive looks if the person next in line edges forward.

2. Create bogus free samples tables. Label the table "Free Samples: Clusterjoys!" Suggested combos: apple with corrugated pickle, sprinkled with Lucky Charms and A1 Sauce. Be creative.

3. Put a GPS on your cart. Consult it and occasionally change direction.

4. While waiting in line to check out, read *Good Housekeeping*, shake your head and huff "Bullshit!" and "Are you fucking kidding me?!" under your breath. Become more emphatic as you read the magazine.

5. Set up a canvas and paint a still life of the produce.

6. Be endlessly picky with your fruit selection. Tap on them. Listen to them. Hold them up to the light. Place them in your pants and bounce up and down. Finally, find the ones you want, then repeat the process with the next produce item.

7. Ask customer service what aisle you can find a) "the green stuff, y'know, the green stuff!" b) "the thing you eat and like it's round," c) "streln." Get increasingly frustrated when they don't understand.

8. Watch the deli slicer and, with each slice, grunt sounds of arousal.

9. Put a small suitcase, open laptop, and your shoes on the checkout counter. Have your passport out.

10. Hide a hamster in your coat pocket. Put a quarter in a gumball dispenser then, using sleight of hand, pull out the hamster.

11. Ask butcher for a) emu b) aardwolf c) "the most human-tasting meat he has."

12. Sneak huffs of cinnamon in the spices aisle. Get caught and then race to put the spice back and pretend to browse items overcasually.

13. Put every item in plastic bags with twisty-ties, including all prepackaged ones. Apologize profusely with a foreign accent to the cashier for misunderstanding. When the cashier finally deals with it, pay in pennies.

14. Fill your cart with hundreds of limes. Wheel around the store, examining other things, but always return to put more limes in the cart. Smile to another patron and say "You just can't beat limes."

15. Enter a frozen foods freezer. When someone opens the door, start blinking your eyes and act like you have awakened in the future. Marvel at the ceiling's "magical firelights." Assume you are in the "Sultan's Palace."

16. Bring additional containers of "toppings" and place them by the salad bar: M&M's, a bowl of dice, Monopoly houses and hotels, etc.

17. By the flower display, leave a picture of a child with "Dedicated to Lisa Mendez 1997-2008." Add candles.

18. Cool off in the vegetable mist machines.

19. Pull your cart with a leash.

20. . . .with someone seated in it dressed as Chinese royalty.

21. Buy 200 sympathy cards and one belated Bar Mitzvah card. Tell the cashier "You don't even want to know what happened."

22. Sing along to the music.

23. Dance along to the music.

24. Devour melons to the music.

25. Unleash the nuts in a bulk section without a bag. Scream, "Jackpot! I'm a winna!"

WHEN THE BALL DROPS
Great Stories in Diarrhea

at the moment of reckoning,

when there is no tomorrow or yesterday,

when the cork comes out of the bottle...

...the ball drops.

⚠ Vulnerability ⚠

This is a story about public diarrhea. But to fully grasp it, you need a little backstory.

I kept telling all my girlfriends, "You gotta try this, this casual dating thing." I would tell them to think of Manhattan men as eligible (or not) for a little something called The Rotation. If found eligible, gentlemen would be told upon entry that there would be no exclusivity, no serious dating, no marriage, etc. In return, you never had to deal with the "games," the wondering, and most importantly, you never ever had to feel vulnerable. The idea was that I'd be in charge, and I called the shots.

"Let's go away for the weekend," he suggested. I panicked. This was not part of The Rotation. You didn't spend 36 hours together in The Rotation. You had a date, then left. But the weekend he suggested sounded so very fun. We would go to Saratoga Springs, watch the horse races, go out to dinner, stay the night, then see his property outside of Woodstock on the way home.

I agreed and packed a particularly cute, white sundress for the occasion. After the races, we went to a small Italian place and ordered everything—salami, mozzarella, pasta in a creamy alfredo sauce, lamb chops dripping with succulent fat, followed by tiramisu and profiteroles for dessert.

The hotel was about a mile from the restaurant, and it was a beautiful night so we decided to walk back. We stopped halfway to get some coffee, and I began to feel some gastric pains. I chalked them up to overeating and didn't worry too much about them. I briefly considered using the restroom, but this was clearly a hippie coffee shop where the key had a big dirty handle on it, and the sink was down the hall. I couldn't be bothered to deal.

As we walked outside the coffee shop, chaos erupted on the streets. It was a street fight between two groups of those notoriously gangster Saratoga Springs teens! The police came, one kid mouthed off to an officer and was taken away in handcuffs. It was all enormously entertaining, and I forgot all about the restroom.

The guy and I continued to walk along home and I was feeling great. We'd had a great day, the guy was really great, and he'd even given me a nice compliment on my lovely white sundress. This weekend was a big deal for me. I hadn't been away with a boy in a couple of years. On that walk I started to think to myself, "Maybe this isn't so bad. Maybe I could imagine slowly opening up, allowing myself to become vulnerable with this guy."

About a quarter mile away from the Marriott, I told the boy I needed to walk a bit more quickly because I really had to pee. Hot coffee sloshing in our stomachs, away we went. Now I could see the Marriott. We were less than 100 yards away. But then it hit me, nearly all at once. I didn't just have to pee. Now the salami, mozzarella, cream sauce, lamb and sweets all combined into an uncontrollable, seconds away, explosive diarrhea.

"Go ahead," I told him, "I'll meet you upstairs in a second." With a quizzical look on his handsome face, he agreed. I was standing with my back to the hotel. I ran through the options in my head. There was a bush nearby but it was a rose bush. I was in my sundress and sandals, sure to be pricked by thorns if I squatted. Then I thought about just standing up and letting it drop. I removed my undies in preparation when I realized that this was a terrible idea. I could tell it was going to be loose and would end up on every inch of my body below the waist. But by that point, it was too late. I let it rip and diarrhea ended up down my legs, on my feet, and even splashed up on to the back of my no longer white sundress. This went on for at least 2 minutes.

When I thought I could depend on a break in the action, I tied my sweater around my waist, covering the back area, I used some rosebush leaves to try and wipe the shit off my legs and feet. I attempted to collect what little dignity I had left, and I walked into the lobby of the Saratoga Marriott. To my horror, the boy was waiting there for me. He had seen the whole thing.

The next steps were obvious, and entailed extensive cleansing, putting the dress in the garbage, and avoiding eye contact for the rest of our time together. I woke up early and felt the need to go for an early morning walk to clear my head, and get a little perspective on what had happened—and tell the groundskeeper about a little unpleasant task he might want to add to his morning rounds. I found him, and gently suggested that he might want to do a little extra cleaning around the rosebushes today.

"Your dog?," he asked.

All I could offer was a sheepish, "Mmm hmm."

And that, my friends, is a little story I like to call "The More You Try to Run From Vulnerability in Your Little White Dress the Sooner it Will Track You Down and Explode All Over You." —Anonymous

Our Forgotten Brothers and Sisters:
Famous People's Less Impressive Siblings

Bill Clinton was elected governor of Arkansas at the age of 32 and went on to become the third youngest president in United States history. During his time in office, he brought peace to the Middle East, restored democracy in Haiti, and enlivened the national economy. Bill's half-brother Roger, by contrast, has a more limited list of accomplishments: he is pretty good at Connect Four, knows the difference between an alligator and a crocodile, and once appeared on the *Ricki Lake* show. And unlike brother Bill, Roger has a dark side. He fights, drinks heavily, and has been addicted to everything from amphetamines to zinc oxide.

We marvel at the discrepancy between the two Clintons, but should we? Is such a disparity between siblings really that rare? Throughout history, many of the world's great minds have grown up with rather unexceptional siblings. Here is a sample of a few of these persons' less than impressive kin.

A Visionary without a Vision

Vincent Van Gogh was the quintessential visionary. Tormented by critics' ignorance, Van Gogh spun a cocoon of introverted anguish. His only true friend was his older brother Theo, whom he considered his soulmate and confidant. Vincent wrote dozens of telling letters during his many years of struggle, and consequently, their relationship is well documented. By contrast, Vincent sent only a few postcards to his younger brother Jerry, and thus there is little account of Jerry Van Gogh in art books and biographies.

Jerry Van Gogh began his career as an accountant, but soon sought his own path in the art world. His early works included *Dirty Sock*, *Boy with Large Genitals* and *Portrait of a Canned Ham*. They excited no one. At the time, brother Vincent questioned the merit of empirical perception and sought a more subjective, more emotional involvement with his art. Jerry faced an intellectual challenge of his own sort, and wrote to Vincent about it:

Dear Vincent,

Art's great quandary soaks my spirit and makes my spirit heavy. In all of my paintings, it is the same. I begin with my subjects' faces and I am happy. But alas, soon I realize I have painted my subjects' faces too low on the canvas, and I have no room to put their legs. I try to play this off by giving my them robot thrusters instead, or making them lizard people, or having them do the splits or something, but it's no use. I am a failure.

Misery engulfs me,

Jerry

P.S. I have begun to eat my paint.

Neither Theo nor Vincent answered Jerry's letters, and he became increasingly despondent. Failure followed failure, until at last, in the footsteps of his brother Vincent, Jerry cut off his ear and sent it to a prostitute. Two months later, he received his ear back in the mail, with "Return to Sender" stamped on the envelope. He had filled out the address incorrectly. This failure would be his last, as shortly thereafter, Jerry starved to death in his shower, unable to circumvent his shampoo bottle's " lather/rinse/repeat" conundrum.

The Unknown Kennedy

The youngest of the five Kennedy boys, Melvin Kennedy was born on July 12, 1937. Unlike brothers John, Robert, and Ted, Melvin was not exceptionally bright. He didn't learn to walk until he was ten, and at the age of fourteen, he knew only a few words: "fruit-cup," "dirt," and "Larry." But the Kennedy's convinced school officials that Melvin's deficiency would not be a major handicap in his communication, because he used his words in creative combinations. This was not the case. Melvin's third grade teacher, Mrs. Ilene Grunspan, described Melvin as "an idiot, dumb as paste... so stupid he couldn't even sit in his chair."

Melvin was neither handsome nor athletic, and had few friends. While the other kids laughed and played outside, Melvin spent most of his free time in the corner, licking the erasers clean. When approached by others, he frowned and hissed at them, warding them off with a "Fruit-cup!" or "Larry!"

During the mid-sixties, Melvin aimed to earn his family name, and pursued a career in politics. Again his limited vocabulary caused problems. By 1965 he had managed to add "elbow" and "possum" to his personal lexicon, which was enough to get him elected mayor of Washington D.C. But less than a year after his inauguration, his office erupted in scandal.

On April 19, 1966, Melvin Kennedy was arrested for illegal use of an overhead projector and was sentenced to two years in prison. Five days later, he committed suicide by swallowing his sheets. His suicide note baffled investigators and reads as follows: "Elbow. Larry dirt possum. Fruit-cup elbow. Larry!"

"You Put the Mess in Messiah!"
Phillip Christ was born in 4 BC to parents Joseph and Mary, the result of a Virgin Cesarean section. He was a happy child and spent his adolescent years woodworking with his little brother Jesus. But as an adult, he was constantly outdone by his younger brother.

It was always "Jesus this, Jesus that" he wrote in his memoirs. "Jesus freed a people today." "Jesus made a lame child walk again." "Jesus! Jesus! Jesus!." But the Virgin Mary made sure to encourage the Jan Brady of Christs, and told Phil if he worked hard, he too could make a good prophet.

So Phil set off alone, in search of enlightenment. He wandered naked in the desert for five years hoping to hear the voice of God. Instead he heard the voice of his Aunt Rita who told him to pick up some vegetables when he was out. Upon his return, Phil was able to amass a small group of followers on the basis of several minor miracles he performed. They were mostly sleight-of-hand tricks he had learned while running three card monte on the street. While he never walked on water, he once put his entire fist in his mouth. When someone suggested he should bear the sins of all people, Phil Christ ran off, saying he had "a cake in the oven," skipped town, and was never seen again.

Other Bumbling Brothers and Sisters:

Rita Plath: After sister Sylvia's glorious suicide, Rita wanted to go out with a bang, too. But she owned no stove, and had to resort to sticking her head in the toaster. She merely "browned" her face a bit, and was often complimented on her healthy tan.

Sammy X: Sammy attempted to duplicate his older brother Malcolm's remarkable act of discipline by reading the dictionary in its entirety. However, he never got very far, and had little appeal as a speaker with his constant irrelevant references to the "aardwolf."

Mohammed Thoreau: Isolation was a fruitful experiment for Henry David Thoreau. Not so, for brother Mo. While Henry compiled myriad observations of nature, pioneered the philosophy of transcendentalism, and scribed thousands of pages in his journal, Mo spent the majority of his time confiding in porno mags. His lone essay, "A Letter to Betty Big Ones," was rejected 183 times before its publication in *Juggs* Magazine.

Dan Juan (pronounced so it rhymes): "The World's Greatest Lover" he was not. Short, fat, and inconsistently toothed, Dan Juan wore substantial headgear and had bad facial acne which he tried to hide with make-up, long hair, or by covering his face with his hands in prolonged feigned amazement. He remained a virgin until his death. But not after.

Frank Gandhi: While Frank had a better build than Mahatma, he did not have his conviction. His own hunger strike lasted about 25 minutes. As a token of support, he did give up nougat for a month.

Tim Gates: By the time Bill Gates invented Windows, Tim Gates hadn't even gotten to Act 2 in Ms. Pac-Man. While Bill went on to realize his vision of what the personal computer could do in society, Tim knew only one computer program:

10 Print

"Tim is cool"

20 Print

Goto 10

Euphemisms for
"I Have to go to the Bathroom"

I have to...

Bake a brownie

Bake a loaf

Bomb the bowl

Choke a brownie

Choke some chocolate

Chop a log

Cook a butt burrito

Cook some chocolate

Crap

Curl some pipe

Defecate

Disembowel

Do the royal squat

Doo-doo

Do the do

Download some brownware

Draw mud

Drop

Drop a bomb

Drop a dookie

Drop a load

Drop anchor

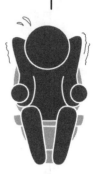

Drop the kids off at the lake

Drop the kids off at the pool

Drop wolf bait

Drop your ordinance

Dump

Dump a stump

Enjoy a meatball sandwich

Evacuate

Evacuate rectally

Give birth to a marine

Hatch a new boss

Hatch a new superintendent

Have a shit

Heave a Havana

Hit paydirt

Launch a torpedo

Lay a brick

Lay a log

Lay some cable

Load the crapper

Make a deposit

Make a doo-doo

Make a log entry

Make mud

Make number two

Make room for lunch

Make some fertilizer

Offload some freight

Pack your underwear

Paint with the brown stuff

Park some bark

Park your breakfast

Pinch a loaf

Poke the turtle's head out

Poo

Poo-poo

Poop

Put fruit in the bowl

Recycle fiber

Release your payload

Ride the hoop

Seek revenge for the brown bomber

Shake a brown bomber

Shit

Shit my brains out

Sink a link

Sink the Bismarck

Sit on the bowl

Sit on the can

Sit on the throne

Snap a log

Spray and wipe

Squat

Squeeze a coily

Squeeze a loaf

Squeeze one out

Taint the cloth

Take a crap

Take a dump

Take a growler

Take a load off your mind

Take a Schroeder

Take a shit

Take a steamer

Take the Browns to the Superbowl

Test the plumbing

Test the toilet

Visit the toilet

Void my bowels

Zap the porcelain

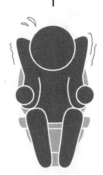

WHEN THE BALL DROPS
Great Stories in Diarrhea

at the moment of reckoning,
when there is no tomorrow or yesterday,
when the cork comes out of the bottle...
...the ball drops.

⚠ **Friends And Enemas** ⚠

It was the summer of 1986. I was 16 years old and a friend of mine was dealing with consistent back pain. Apparently, his family had a history of kidney problems, so they wanted to check him out in more detail. He was scheduled for a barium enema. He was a little freaked out, I guess I would have been as well, and he asked if I would go with him.

We sat in the waiting area of a rather small office, surprised the procedure wasn't taking place at a hospital. He went into the testing area not too far from where I was waiting. I watched television, read magazines, and fell asleep over the course of the next hour until I heard a loud voice announce, "Look out, I am gonna blow!!!!"

I had absolutely zero knowledge of what was going on in the other room, and was startled. But after a minute, I turned my attention back to whatever I was watching. Ten minutes later, my friend came out of the room, finished his paperwork, and we left.

As we got in the car and drove home, I noticed a stench. The kind of stench that gets worse every second. The kind of stench that, even when you opened the window, only gets worse. As we were not near any farms, I finally ask my friend if he had "cleared his throat" as it were. That's when I noticed something that I was certain was the cause of the foul aroma, but I still couldn't believe my eyes.

"What's that on your pants?" I asked.

Then he explained to me the events of the past hour. He told me that after he got into the room, they gave him what tasted like a sports drink. I assumed that was the barium. Then he sat there for a half an hour undressed until it was time to get on all fours.

Now remember, we were both 16 years old, still somewhat of an awkward age to be getting on all fours knowing that someone is going to jam a tube in your chocolate starfish. He described the experience as, "not the most pleasant thing he ever experienced, but not brutal, until they turned on the juice."

That he described as, "having a couple of gallons of water slammed up there. It just made me feel really bloated." He sat there with a tube in is his scrunchy for about another 15-20 minutes. He thought the worst was over. The nurse came in and told him she'd be removing the tube. As she did so, he got that feeling. You know, that rumble that a stomach makes only when things inside are not well. He knew immediately what was going to happen and wanted to warn everyone in its path. But it was too late. As the tube made its exit, his scream ("Look out, I am gonna blow!!!!") echoed through the room and was followed by a fludderblast of material that would make even a sewer worker pass out. Like a hurricane, it took out everything including the nurse, the table, the wall, the sink, the door, and unfortunately, his clothes. He said it looked like the Jolly Green Giant had a taken a jolly sized ketchup packet and stomped on it. Only it was filled with poop.

He went on to explain that the nurse was very kind, even though she made sure to tell him that this was the worst "blowout" she had ever witnessed. She helped him clean off his stuff, but in all the excitement, they had missed some.

As he finished his story, I tried to stop laughing because a) I felt bad, but more importantly 2) I was trying not to inhale the stench that was growing and taking over the car like the evil empire. When we finally arrived at our destination, I could plainly see that all of his "sports drink" had not been properly disposed of and was still drooling out of him as we drove home. Not only was it evident on his pants, socks, and shoes, but also on the lovely cloth seats of his 1982 Ford Escort as well. It was not a pretty sight. My friend, and the car for that matter, would never be the same again. And in case you were wondering, the tests were negative. No kidney problems. Just a pulled muscle... —TL

MindF*cks:
6 Things to Do at Museums

1. Convince onlookers that a Jackson Pollock painting is actually 3-D Magic Eye Art, and that if they stare long enough, an image will appear.

2. Scratch and sniff paintings featuring food.

3. Bring your own sketch of a tree to the Met. Put it on the floor, then tell the guard "I think this fell down."

4. At a modern art museum, admire the coat rack or museum map with knowing nods. See if others follow.

5. Put $9.99 price tag on Picassos.

6. At a wax museum, resculpt Princess Diana's face so that she looks like Kurt Rambis.

Behind The Music:
The Chicago Bears Shufflin' Crew
By Eric Immerman

Narrator:

It all began as a charitable endeavor. Ten gridiron warriors who wanted to make music. Not because they were greedy, but rather, to feed the needy. Fusing innovative rap with what could only be described as interpretive dance, they ascended to the top of the charts with the 1985 hit single, "Super Bowl Shuffle." Tonight, we go inside the huddle and behind the music with The Chicago Bears Shufflin' Crew.

Onstage, they were arrogant and brash, a group so bad they knew they were good, frequently blowin' your mind like they knew they would. But offstage, things were falling apart, as band mates began questioning the ability of lead singer and songwriter, Speedy Willie Gault.

[Lead guitarist] "Samurai" Mike Singletary:

Take, for example, the lyric "We're not here to start no trouble." It blatantly contained a double negative, leaving us confused as to whether or not we were there to start trouble. I love Willie, but as a lyricist, he wasn't as gifted, as say, a Bob Dylan or Allen Iverson.

Narrator:

While the band struggled with ambiguous lyrics, frontman Willie Gault felt he was sacrificing artistic integrity for commercial success.

"Speedy" Willie Gault:

As a songwriter, I felt like I was suffocating. The only tune people wanted to hear was "Super Bowl Shuffle." I mean, no one ever requested my dark, brooding ballad about Buddy Ryan's vaunted 46-zone defense.

Narrator:

But the band soon discovered there was an even more perilous underbelly to fame and fortune, as morbidly obese saxophonist William "Refrigerator" Perry fell victim to temptation, and, ultimately, addiction.

William "Fridge" Perry:

I was out of control. I was a junkie. After one late-night Pringles binge my cholesterol level was so high that I almost...[starts crying]. I should've known better. I may be large, but I'm no dumb cookie.

Narrator:

Things were spiraling downwards for the Crew and they were about to hit rock bottom.

[Mama's Boy] Otis Wilson:

We were supposed to open for Culture Club and there was no way we could go on. Punky QB Jim McMahon was wearing just his shades and a strategically placed headband with the message "Rozelle Sucks" written on it; Speedy Willie refused to sing unless we introduced him as "Chocolate Swirl"; and Singletary was juiced up on lattes and his eyes were shifting violently from side to side. It was intense.

Narrator:

Despite their troubles the band forged ahead. However, their follow-up album—an instrumental effort called "Intentional Grounding"—alienated their loyal fan base and failed to crack the Top 40. Suddenly, one of the most successful bands of the 1980s was relegated to playing Bar Mitzvahs in suburban Chicago.

[Punky QB] Jim McMahon:

Do you know how hard it was to keep the yarmulke on my spiked hair?

Narrator:

The lukewarm reception to their second album, combined with the incessant infighting between McMahon and backup singer Steve Fuller, eventually led to the band's breakup in December of 1991. Fuller embarked on a solo career. Perry co-founded popular rap trio The Fat Boys. And Richard Dent went on to a career in choreography, with famous clients such as NBA star Mark Madsen.

But the Shufflin' Crew's legacy would prove to be an enduring one. Their innovative dance moves spawned the infectious "Ickey Shuffle," and their complex rhyming schemes can be heard today on such industry staples as "Shaq Fu: Da Return."

And now, ten years after their breakup stunned the music world, The Chicago Bears Shufflin' Crew are reuniting for a benefit concert. Fans across the country are brimming with excitement.

Fan:

I'm stoked they're getting back together. You haven't seen anything until you've seen Gary Fencik play the keyboards live!

Narrator:

And so the Shufflin' Crew has come full circle and are now back together doing what they do best...struttin' for fun, struttin' their stuff for everyone.

[Fade to black]

The World's Worst... Professional Wrestlers

The Fact Checker

The object of anathema for many blue collar fans, the Fact Checker, whose tights feature excerpts from Harper's, constantly bores the fans by slightly correcting the catchphrase-riddled bellows of his opponents. Nemesis: The Assistant Editor.

The Orthodontist

Performs bridgework after pinfall. If pinned, he allows opponents to choose a toy from a special drawer. Moves: the root canal, the retainer. Dental hygienist valet often distracts opponents, at which time he'll use one of the many dental tools he has laid out for intimidation purposes before the match.

The Guru (Internet Start-up CEO)

Pseudo casual demeanor belies ferocious competitive streak, which surfaces when tested; uses business clichés like "the nature of the beast"; "on the radar screen"; and "Proactive Paradigm" in his trash-talking rhetoric. Foreign objects include Koosh balls, troll dolls, and vortex footballs.

The Freudian Grappler

Mercilessly sedates opponents, then as they lie exhausted and reclined, gets them to confess traumatic childhood experiences that are the root of their violence. Broke with his former tag-team partner, Dr. Jungblood, over disagreements on crowd psychology. Jungblood was a firm believer in the archetypal desire for people to chant USA, USA, USA no matter what nation the wrestlers are from.

The Leper

Repulses foes with contagious open sores, often winning by count-out. Tights—thong.

Ali the Muslim

Unfortunate scheduling during Ramadan forces the Muslim to have to wrestle while always facing Mecca. Fans cheer by making that weird sound, you know what I'm talking about. That sound.

The Morning DJ

Theme music is BTO's "Ain't Seen Nothing Yet"; communicates in amazingly and annoyingly loud exuberant speech. "Boink"ing and other silly sounds accompany his punches.

The Incontinent Enforcer

Self-explanatory.

The Logical Positivist

Self-explanatory.

The Sales Representative

Occupation does not come into play in any way during wrestling.

Next Caller

If you don't have time to form your own, whip out the opinion at the next cocktail party you attend:

I Support the War but Not the Troops

I'm not saying our fighting men and women aren't brave. But every military guy I've known says the bulk of the other guys are idiots and douchebags. That being said, like it or not, replacing dictatorships with democracy in the Middle East is an arguably admirable goal even if there are US casualties. There is more to the world than American lives. We need to care about them too. Next caller.

WHEN THE BALL DROPS
Great Stories in Diarrhea

at the moment of reckoning,
when there is no tomorrow or yesterday,
when the cork comes out of the bottle...
...the ball drops.

⚠ The Diarrhea Cockblock ⚠

It was a Friday night in Deal, New Jersey. I was walking toward my friend Jamie's house in the dark when I saw his neighbor, a cute girl I'd had my eye on. She had an incredible body with a small waist, curvy ass, and perfect big breasts. She was also extremely flirty. I told Jamie that at some point I'd have to see if I could get in her pants.

The girl and I started to talk and began walking toward Ocean Avenue. The conversation was going extremely well and in the right direction. The next thing I know we're talking about sexual positions we wanted to try and what kinds of kinky things we had experimented with. I was so focused on the task at hand that I didn't realize that an hour had passed. I also didn't realize how badly I had to go to the bathroom—until I started cramping while we walked along. I stopped for a minute and told her that I had "pulled" a stomach muscle that day and that walking had aggravated it. This happened twice more before I realized that I was in serious trouble.

Suddenly, the realization hit me: I HAD TO GO TO THE BATH-ROOM REALLY BADLY AND I MIGHT NOT MAKE IT. I told her, "I'm in a lot of pain. Let's head back." You might ask yourself, "How did I let this go so far?" Well, between the first and second cramps she started demonstrating yoga poses for me, showing me all kinds of interesting ways she could contort herself. Then, between cramps two and three, she asked me to help her into a pose where she bent all the way back and had her hands touch the ground with her feet on the floor and those gorgeous tits pointing straight up in my face. I'm thinking the whole time that I'm getting laid tonight for sure.

Anyway, now I'm in trouble. When I started visibly sweating I knew I couldn't make it back home. I could only think of two options: 1) The Deal temple, which was a half a block in one direction or 2) my friend Marty's house, which was half a block in the other direction. I knew I could make both. I decided on Marty's house for fear that the temple might be locked. As we walked that way, my mind was racing and I was walking funny trying to hold it in. We got to the house and I made a dash for the front door. I told the girl to wait outside.

As I got up onto the porch, I felt a little squirt come out. I was freaking out inside. I knocked on the door, no answer. Another squirt came but I thought if someone let me in now, it could be OK. I knocked again, nothing. The girl called to me from the street, "Is everything OK?"

I told her I was heading to the back for a minute and she should wait for me on the sidewalk. I ran towards the backyard and I lost it. I could feel the shit start to leak down my leg. Now I was panicked. There were lights on in the back-yard and there was no place I could finish my crap without being illuminated for the whole world to see.

Squirt, squirt. More shit came running down my leg when I uncrossed my legs. Finally, I rushed to a dark spot, dropped my shorts and let it fly. I didn't realize at first that the place I had chosen to make a deposit was right at the bottom of the children's metal slide.

My shorts and legs were stained and wet, I was still in pain, and now I was consumed with this incredible fear of getting caught shitting in the back of a good friend's house at the bottom of his slide or by this girl who 20 minutes ago looked like a cinch to at least blow me.

I tried to muster up the mental energy to finish my business but I couldn't find anything to wipe with. I tried a leaf but it cracked upon contact and I ended up getting shit on my hand and making a bigger mess. I searched the ground and finally found a Kit Kat candy wrapper. Then I heard the girl whispering my name, loudly. She was making her way to the backyard!

I shoved the wrapper up my ass and wiped as best I could, which wasn't very well. I pulled my shorts up and told her to wait for me around the front. I looked myself over quickly. Mercifully, it's dark in Deal because there are no street lamps. And I blessed the mayor of Deal, who I spent years making fun of for being cheap and for not putting more lights around town. I ran towards the girl, put my hands up and told her, "Don't come too close. I stepped in shit back there."

We walked home 15 feet apart from each other, waving goodnight from a distance. Did she know what really happened? To tell you the truth, I don't know. We never spoke about it and soon afterward she began a relationship with the guy she eventually married. At some point, I heard she became very religious. I ran into her a couple of times after that, and I imagine she was probably ashamed about our discussion and what might have happened that night had I not imploded. —Anonymous

 TOILET TRIVIA

Queen Elizabeth I had a portable box-shaped toilet covered with red velvet and trimmed in lace.

The 7 Most Important People Under 7!

Whitney Houston once boldly postulated that the children are our future, an assertion that was later proven with flow charts. Here then, are the children, the future, the faces and minds that will be running and influencing our world in the next millennium. Like all lists of this ilk, we have assembled a list highlighting a diversity of careers and talents, pretending that artists and non-computer people still matter in this world.

Lawrence Neller, Age 6, Artist

Neller, a groundbreaking artist who works primarily in the medium of crayon and pastel, commanded over $600,000 per piece at Sotheby's last summer. Comparisons have already been made to Van Gogh, who like Lawrence, often indulged in consuming many of his art supplies. Neller's most accomplished drawings include *My Trip to the Zoo*, *Boy with Big Head*, and *Untitled 63*, which brilliantly depicts a smiling sun in the corner, flanked by birds represented by minimalist "m"s. One critic described *63* as an "innovative hybrid of neodadaistic surrealism and retro-impressionism." When asked about this, Neller said, "My favorite colors are periwinkle and brick red."

"Freddie", Age 5, Internet Entrepreneur

Freddie (last name withheld per his request) is poised to be the Internet's foremost purveyor of porn, designing and running over 200 websites, which through expensive memberships, grant subscribers thousands of jpeg, mpeg, and avi files. Freddie, who personally finds girls and sex "icky," offers among other lewd, sometimes deviant postings: "Big-Breasted Three-Way," "Sandra Bullock's Secret Sex Video," "Woman Gets Donkey-Punched By Edward R. Murrow," "Woman Has Sex With Elf at Macy's," "Nude Photos Of Madeline Albright!," "John Madden Fists Pat Summeral," "Jennifer Love Hewitt Speaks

Yiddish!," "Aquaman And Green Lantern Snuggling," "Amish Barn-raising Orgy," and "Pam Anderson And Former NFL Commissioner Pete Rozelle Sex Tapes!"

Michelle Bautista, Age VI, Activist

Michelle's first organized protest was a boycott of her school's Salisbury steak; she demanded a vegetarian alternative, and the use of more ecological non-Styrofoam trays. She went on to launch nationwide campaigns against public school involvement with the Pledge of Allegiance, which violates the separation of Church and State, the song "Rudolph the Red Nosed Reindeer," which "preaches tolerance of abnormality based only on its utilitarian value," and the Arabic number system, which she says originated in an ultra-patriarchal society that stifles the development of women. Michelle, who writes speeches for the ACLU, has absolutely no friends.

Cindy Johnston, Age 4, Model, Actress

By the age of two, Cindy was already a veteran in the commercial industry, pitching baby foods, diapers, and acting as the face-girl for a popular children's aspirin. She has won numerous pageants including Miss Little America 1999, Miss Toddler USA 1997, and Miss Pedophile Fodder 1998. Cindy's parents recently negotiated a sitcom development deal for their daughter, which she found unsatisfactory. After breaking with her parents professionally (they are still amicable in their personal lives), Cindy, with the help of Creative Artists Agency, inked a $20 million five-picture deal and recorded a double platinum cover version of "Whoomp, There It Is."

Reggie, Larry, or Tim (still debating) Warga, Age 0, Athlete

While the name has yet to be decided, 6'8", 245-pound Lars and 6'4" Wilma (Lars wed her for breeding purposes), have no doubt about the potential of their genetically enhanced progeny-to-be. Early sonograms show development far beyond average both in physicality and in the medulla oblongata, the area of the brain linked to coordination and dexterity. The New York Mets and Utah Jazz have already expressed interest for the strapping young fetus who, computers project, will throw a fastball of over 100 miles per hour, run a four minute mile, and be able to grow charismatic facial hair.

Raul Gurevich, Age 7, Poet, Depressed Genius

In the first grade, when asked how he wanted his kickball pitch, Raul responded with the peculiar, "flaccid and sullen." School psychologists noted that Raul's social awkwardness and listless, depressed demeanor were clearly linked to his moving, emotionally stunning poetry and prose. They urged his parents to encourage their son's genius with constant discouragement and by providing an unhealthy, dysfunctional home environment full of marital turmoil and domestic abuse. By age 7, Raul was writing dark pessimistic work comparable to Hemmingway and Plath. Raul takes metasizin daily, an anti-anti-depressant to keep his outlook bleak and meaningful.

Melvin DeHart, Age 5 1/2 , Musician, Composer

The world's foremost woodblock virtuoso, Melvin D. has mesmerized audiences throughout North America and Europe with his enchanting rhythms and expert mallet-work. From his haunting, ominous "Tah-Tah-Ti-Ti-Tah," to the subtle-then-ecstatic "Ti-Ti-Ti-Tah-Tah," Melvin can tap into the emotional experience with his mallet and stained slab of oak like no other. Melvin's parents, Sarah, a professor of Art History, and William, a biomedical researcher, encourage their son's gift by mandating 7 hours of practice a day, threatening that if he does not comply, he will be beaten with a willow twig and forced to eat eggplant and weeds for a week.

Job Wanted

TATTOOINE: As the effects of the lagging economy ripple throughout space and time, bail enforcement agents, more commonly known as "bounty hunters" are finding it difficult to locate clients. "Paying someone just to hunt someone down is a luxury service," explains Greedo, a freelance bounty hunter who owns his own business, and now has taken a second job as an Ewok day care worker. Greedo is not the only freelancer being forced to repurpose his resumé.

Curriculum Vitae
BOBA FETT, C.P.A
Kamino
(Beyond Outer Rim,
Just South of Rishi Maze)

Objective

Faceless enforcer with demonstrated initiative and good time-management seeks accounting position

Qualifications

· IMA Certified

· Distinctive armor strikes fear in the hearts of fugitives

· All business, laconic, and deadly

·Preeminent bounty hunter of the galaxy

·Working knowledge of Quicken, Excel, and Carbonite Freezing procedures

Experience

President/CEO, Fett Bail Enforcement Agency (Long, Long Ago to Present)

· Managed, developed, and maintained all aspects of finance, accounting, foreign exchange dealings, marketing, and data processing for private bail enforcement agency (40,000 Altarian credits annually); oversaw offices on Tattooine and Hoth

· Captured Han Solo and crew of Millenium Falcon

Experience *continued*	· Tracked down a Rebel agent known as "Mole" on the frozen world of Ota
	· Plunged into Sarlacc pit beast; kept alive by numerous fibrous suckers that attached themselves to my body as part of the Sarlacc's horrible metabolic process (it would keep its prey alive for thousands of years, all the while slowly feeding off it); almost lost identity in the swirling dementia brought about by the Sarlacc's toxins; used EE3 Blaster Rifle and whipcord lanyard launcher to get free of the beast
	· Prepared financial statements and schedules
	Wookie Pimp
	· Built consumer deviant behavior models for corporate clients using multivariate techniques, including regression and discriminant analysis
	· Generated 200,000 credits with aggressive prospecting campaign on Ewok moon planet of Endor
	· Subcontracted gay robots
Hobbies	· Working on my ship (Slave I) · Avenging the death of father · Crossword puzzles · I like to wear several ominous braids that hang from my shoulder (trophies from fallen prey that underscore my lethality)
References	All dead

WHEN THE BALL DROPS
Great Stories in Diarrhea

at the moment of reckoning,
when there is no tomorrow or yesterday,
when the cork comes out of the bottle...

...the ball drops.

⚠ Seven-Oops ⚠

In my senior year of high school, I was lucky enough to attend a traveling school where you visited a foreign country for a month for credit. We were hiking in the Copper Canyons of Mexico, home to the Tarahumara Indians who are famous for their ability to run for days at a time.

Well, there was only one thing running in our group—and that was an endless flow of diarrhea and puke. On one back country truck ride, my teacher spewed fresh enchilada vomit all over my backpack. I was horrified. I knew I wasn't his favorite student but I still had to wonder why my backpack was chosen for cheesy coverage when it was sitting next to 20 other perfectly good options.

Our student body president was named Brick. Brick was a clean cut young man whose life dream was to enter the U.S. Air Force Academy. Even brave Brick was laid low by the food and water situation in this unfamiliar land. At one point, he was using one of the few outhouses we came across—a step up from the holes in the ground we'd been forced to use at times. As we all waited in line, we heard a loud noise, somewhere between a scream and a squeal. Apparently, Brick had ingested so much Pepto Bismol during his time south of the border that his excrement had turned into a chunky, hot pink stream. No joke.

I laughed with the arrogance of a fool. I felt smug and superior. I was the only person in our group of 15 who had not fallen pray to the shits while in Mexico. "Suckers!" I thought to myself, "I am strong! VIVA AMERICA!"

And then we got to Mexico City.

It was our last day, and we were finally in civilization—meaning we had a toilet that actually flushed. My luck had run out. I felt piercing pain tearing apart my insides until I shed tears. I stayed on the bowl for hours—emptying out every drop of liquid I could muster. And then one more. I was so dehydrated my lips were cracking—but I didn't care.

I slept wrapped around that toilet on the dirty, cold, porcelain of a Mexican hotel bathroom until "the Doctor" could see me. I later discovered that he was not a doctor at all, just the guy down at the pharmacy working the front desk that day.

"EVERYONE OUT! OUT !!! WE MUST HAVE PRIVACY!" He shooed everyone into the hall and I was ready to be saved. He lifted my shirt ever so lightly above my belly button and pressed on my stomach for a minute, sucking his teeth and shaking his head. "YOU EAT BAD FOOD" was his diagnosis. "Yes," I said. "Yes."

He pushed his hand hard into my gut for what seemed like an eternity and said, in heavily accented broken English, "A ha! You have problem in your stomach. Yes, you do. I fix you. Take these pills and you must a drink a fifteen seven -ooops."

Seven-oops? Then I figured it out.

"Fifteen 7 Ups? You must mean fifteen sips of 7 Up? I mean, I can't even hold down spit, let alone a soda."

"Eh, no, no. Must have fifteen 7-ooops."

He proceeded to line up 15 7-ups alongside the nightstand while my classmates waited patiently in the hallway. It was ominous, like a marathon I was supposed to run after not training even one little bit. He shoved one of those old green bottles towards my mouth. I reluctantly drank it as he encouraged me.

As the first sip of fizzy liquid hit the back of my throat, my intestines went into full on revolt. I raised myself out of bed and ran buck naked in front of my entire high school class. I didn't make it back to the porcelain room. As I ran, I simultaneously puked and pooped all over myself.

I am not sure exactly what the view from behind me looked like—brown and runny no doubt—but a vision of it briefly crossed my mind as I looked out into the crowd and gave my graduation speech a few weeks later. I fought hard to push it away.

No one ever spoke of Mexico again after we got back home. Except for the school nurse, who called me in to report that the pills the Mexican "doctor" had given me were old urinary tract infection medicine that had been outlawed in America 15 years ago. —CS

 TOILET TRIVIA

Constipation occurs when the large intestine absorbs too much water.

Pornification

Genre Edition

For every movie, there exists, at least theoretically, a porno version of that movie. Can you "pornify" the titles below?

Comedy

Legally Blonde

O' Brother Where Art Thou?

Mary Poppins

Roger & Me

Broadcast News

Analyze This

The Breakfast Club

Network

Young Frankenstein

Office Space

Napoleon Dynamite

Drama

Malcolm X

Good Will Hunting

Vanilla Sky

Monster's Ball

Se7en

Six Degrees of Separation

Waiting to Exhale

Fear and Loathing in Las Vegas

(Answers on page 146)

Pornification

(Answer Key for the quiz on page 145)

Comedy:

Legally Blonde = Barely Legally Blonde

O' Brother Where Art Thou? = O' Brothel, Where Art Thou?

Mary Poppins = Cherry Poppin'

Roger & Me = Rogerin' Me

Broadcast News = Broadcast Spews

Analyze This = Analize This

The Breakfast Club = The Fake Breast Club

Network = Nutwork

Young Frankenstein = Hung Frankenstein

Office Space = Orifice Space

Napoleon Dynamite = Napoleon Sodomite

Drama:

Malcolm X = Malcolm XXX

Good Will Hunting = Good Will Humping

Vanilla Sky = Vanilla Eye

Monster's Ball = Monster Balls

Se7en = SeXen, Ei8ht

Six Degrees of Separation = Six Degrees Of Penetration

Waiting to Exhale = Waiting to Impale, Waiting to Inhale

Fear and Loathing in Las Vegas = Queer and Blowing in Las Vegas

TOILET TRIVIA

The average office desk has 400 times more bacteria than a toilet.

Facts That Sound For a Second Like They Might Be True But Aren't

Footnotes are called such because early Greek philosophers wrote them on the bottoms of their feet to hide their true sources of their presentations.

Koalas are known to stalk and kill kangaroos.

The people in sample photos placed in picture frames and wallets are political prisoners whose services are not paid for, but rather mandated.

The Atlanta Falcons helmet is modeled after a doodle in Isaac Newton's notebook.

5 o'clock shadow is actually worst at 7 o'clock.

In Uruguay, children give candy to adults on Halloween as they trick or treat.

Lightning always strikes people in the hip or shin.

The chemical activated in the brain during sex is also found in English muffins.

A chef's hat is called a "pleln."

Last year, the most popular name in China was Wendell.

The word "corndog" is used twice in the Bible.

On average, it takes 300 licks to get to the middle of Tootsie Pop. 400 for Jews.

Richard Dawson gave 11 contestants mouth herpes during his tenure as host on *Family Feud*.

A sixth Marx Brother, Wilfred, did not have a sense of humor and was a realtor.

The Great Gatsby was originally titled *What's Happenin'?*

Statistically, billiards is America's deadliest sport.

The walrus urinates inward. That's what it's doing when it makes that noise.

The first keyboard only had the 14 "most popular" letters.

Frederick Douglass slept with a magnifying glass in his pillow.

The horseshoe crab defecates 24 times its weight every day.

Air Guitar will be an Olympic event in the 2012 Summer Olympics.

The cartoon *Tom and Jerry* was originally written as an allegory of World War II.

Waffles have indentations on them because on Hanukkah the fleeing Jewish people did not have enough batter to make them fully rectangular.

Bill Gates cannot see the color purple. He attributes his success to this fact.

Your mouth produces 46 liters of saliva each day.

We have a few taste buds on the backs of our hands.

The sentence "Six large hogs smoked a salmon" contains every letter in the English alphabet.

Sparrows kill more people per year than bears.

Home plate is shaped as a pentagon because baseball has Satanic roots.

The reason golf balls have dimples is so they will not appear as nuts to rodents.

The reason John Hancock signed the Declaration of Independence so large is because he had hands twice the size of a normal human being.

Tennis courts were originally built at a 15 degree angle so stronger players could play weaker ones and make the match even.

18 scrotums for the wombat.

Propostion 56: Golf Course/Cemeteries Land Preservation Act

With the numbers of both recreational golfers and the deceased growing exponentially, and as real estate consumes more and more of the American wilderness,
there simply isn't enough land for both additional golf courses and more grave sites
for the dead. This measure introduces legislation that would decree state and local
governments to combine cemeteries and golf courses into one property. Mourners
should of course be wary of stray balls, and accordingly, golfers should ask permis-
sion to "play through" a funeral. Headstones and open graves (sand traps) make for
challenging obstacles.

Proposition 35: Coolness Limit on Graphics Initiative Statute

This measure places strict and universal limits on the levels of complexity, realism
and "coolness" as defined by the state (*Terminator 2* vs. Kentucky, 1996) to that of
pre-1985 entertainment consoles, excluding Intellivision. The idea is that nobody
can associate these video games with reality. "Who is going to hurl a ball at a bunch
of colored stripes?" ask the crafters of this legislation, alluding to Atari's *Break Out*.
"*Warlords* is a game about violence, but was violence caused in its wake? Of course
not. Violence on waterways actually decreased after the unveiling of *River Raid* in
1983."

Proposition 32: Condom Expiration Date Eradication Act

This proposal outlaws the printing of expiration dates on condoms in order to
save males from the humiliation of throwing expired condoms away. While the
measure will likely spread disease and unwanted pregnancies, proponents of the
bill argue that this is not enough to offset the shame caused by said act.

Proposition 15: Midgets as Pets

This measure allows for the abduction and exploitation of midgets and dwarves for personal affection and entertainment.

Proposition 56: Landmarks for paintball wars act

This proposition amends current legislation regarding national landmarks and monuments to allow the federal government to rent these spaces out for the expressed purposes of paintball wars. A sport of unchecked growth and profitability, paintball provides fun for all ages. Monuments mentioned in the proposition are The Capitol (during session), Mount Rushmore, and the National Gallery of Art.

Proposition 32: Revision of TV rating system

This measure amends current FCC rating standards. No longer will they be allowed to show breasts on TV if they belong to a woman of a primitive tribe sporting diseased, flabby breasts with a wooden peg through the nipple. Nor will women's breasts be shown freely on medical shows. No more will the "As long as the breasts are unattractive they can be shown" rule apply. The romantic comedy will also have warnings on them in the form of a NR rating (not realistic) as they preach that the way to a woman's heart is to annoy them with sardonic witty barbs which eventually charm her into realizing that she does in fact love you.

 TOILET TRIVIA

The reason corn appears in our feces has more to do with evolution than digestion. Back in the caveman days, we had larger molars and could chew plant material—ie, corn—more thoroughly. As we evolved, our teeth got smaller and things like whole kernels of corn started to appear whole in our stools.

The Bar-Mitzvah

The Bar-Mitzvah was a fiasco. No one was mingling, everyone was in a lousy mood, and the band didn't know "Celebration" or "Shout." The kids were restless—where was the magician? The older crowd was complaining it was too cold and minutes earlier, Sadie Abromowitz had had an allergic reaction to the lox spread. But Jeffrey, the Bar-Mitzvah boy, couldn't have cared less. For Jeffrey's peculiar Uncle Saul had been giving him sips of his bourbon all through the night...... You pick the ending!

1. Maybe that explains why Jeffrey is an alcoholic now.

2. When Jeffrey awoke, he was on a ship steaming towards Bolivia, and the wonderful world of white slavery.

3. Then the bomb went off. Fire swept the hall and debris cluttered the room. There were no survivors—well maybe a few, but they were so maimed and disfigured they're not worth mentioning.

4. After Jeffrey vomited on his grandmother, they took him to the hospital to have his stomach pumped. Now the whole family drinks.

5. No one really knows for sure what happened next, but Uncle Saul insists they were just "snuggling."

THE DIARRHEA MONOLOGUES

WHEN THE BALL DROPS
Great Stories in Diarrhea

at the moment of reckoning,

when there is no tomorrow or yesterday,

when the cork comes out of the bottle...

...the ball drops.

⚠ Incident on 34th Street ⚠

My wife, a recent vegetarian who had just graduated from nutritional school, convinced me that my meat-coated colon had to be cleansed. Three months previously, I had joined a formal collection of like-minded beer and burger fanatics and had set out to sample 100 of the best burgers in New York City. Needless to say, my carnivore ways were getting the best of my otherwise regular bowel movements. Her recommendation: a colonic.

It was a seasonably warm July day when I set out on my mountain bike for the ride from our apartment to the doctor's office in midtown. I was wearing a loose fitting t-shirt and tan shorts—an old pair of work khakis that had been recycled for summer use. A convenient 20-minute bike ride from my apartment, the midtown location was ideal.

The nondescript office was clean yet small. I was immediately struck at the uncanny similarity in appearance my colonisist had with my 1st grade teacher, Mrs. Harrington. An attractive woman in her early 30s, my 1st grade doppelganger led me into a bathroom directly next to the reception area. I immediately noticed a long cushioned board on the top of the bathtub. I was told to lay naked on the board and immediately thought of a recent article I had read on the controversial CIA interrogation practice of water boarding. My heart started to beat fast and I felt a creeping anxicty.

The specifics of the procedure were simple enough. A lubricated metal tipped hose was inserted into my rectum while a seemingly endless stream of warm saline water was pumped into my small and large intestines. During this process, my colonisist massaged my lower abdominal region and asked me to "relax."

After an awkward 40 minutes, I was told to sit on the toilet, with my legs elevated on a stool, and to release the excessive water. Looking at me directly, the colonisist firmly told me, "You will initially feel a sudden surge of water release but should stay here for at least 30 minutes to make sure that everything gets out."

Alone in the room, I felt initial release of what seemed to be a substantial quantity of liquid but I soon realized that the situation was not conducive towards my psychological bathroom needs. The foot-traffic outside the door could have been bearable, and the sandpaper-like toilet paper in the office could have been bearable, but I had nothing to read and that combined with those other obstacles made the experience impossible. I figured it wouldn't be a problem. After all, my apartment, with privacy, my magazines and my soft toilet paper was only a 20-minute bike ride away.

Approaching the receptionist to pay for the colonic service, my colonisist immediately approached me, concerned. She practically ordered me to return to the bathroom. In a tone of half-panic I replied that I was fine, that I NEEDED to leave NOW. Exasperated, she merely shrugged her shoulders, let out a small huff, and walked away. I had exact change, $70—$60 for the colonic fee and a $10 tip. I laughed to myself. It was a small fee to pay to allow my 1st grade teacher look-alike to insert a metal object and hose up my rectum. Outside, I hopped on my bike and started my way down 5th Avenue—glad to breathe the fresh air, free from the shackles of the hose.

It is important to keep in mind that the events in the following three paragraphs occurred in the course of approximately three seconds. The corner of 34th and 5th is directly in front of the iconic Empire State Building. To my left was The Graduate Center, the doctoral granting college of the City University of New York. Stopped at the light, with my left foot sturdy on the pavement, my right on the pedal, I felt a small rumble in the bottom of my stomach. The best way to describe the sensation would be that of a small bubble of gas, what I might refer to as a 'tiny fart.' In other words, it seemed to me that the gas about ready to leave my colon was nothing monumental, white-knuckle worthy, or offensive. Instinctively, I wanted to expel the small gas bubble so I repositioned my ass two or three inches upward—a normal and innate gesture that I had done countless times in my life to allow optimal gas flow.

Deceivingly, that 'small gas bubble' was, in fact, at least a gallon of warm brown water that proceeded to shoot out of my ass with the velocity of a high-powered ballistic missile, immediately filling my khaki-converted shorts and running down my legs and onto the pavement, forming a small puddle of post-colonic discharge on the mid-town asphalt. At this very moment—in 10ths of seconds, incalculable to the average human sense of time, I heard in a loud voice these three words: WHAT THE FUCK!!

Looking over my right shoulder, there was, not even four feet behind me, a very large and muscular bike messenger. Though physically intimidating, his facial expression was far from aggressive. With a look of shock, intimidation, perhaps even fear, he stared at me. Looking forward and taking a deep breath, the instinct of flight took hold and I immediately ran the red light. Not caring for my physical safety or the sound of motorists or cabbies cursing at me I set my sights forward, not looking back, trying to achieve one goal—the East River. There I would be safe from the scrutiny of society and have a straight shot for home and the security of my own bathroom with my own magazines.

The next 20 minutes felt like an eternity. I constantly looked behind me, was the messenger biker following me? Was he going to demand an explanation? Or was he still "drop jawed" on the corner of 34th and 5th in shock at what he just saw?

I read once that when a traumatic event occurs, people will often repress the experience and keep it to themselves, often leading to future psychological disorders. Fearing such a disorder I set out, after a lengthy shit, shower, and change of clothes, to my regular pub where I proceeded to tell friends and strangers alike about my colonic experience. Two years have passed since the incident, and to this day I am often asked to repeat the story.

Though I initially felt like a victim, I now realize that the real victim was the unfortunate bike messenger who happened upon my path that afternoon. I occasionally think to myself, how did he come to terms with what he saw? Did his friends and family believe him? To this day when I am in mid-town Manhattan and see a bike messenger I instinctively tense up. Will he recognize me? I have decided that if he does recognize me I will offer to buy him a beer at my favorite pub and tell him the story of the Incident on 34th Street. —MTZ

 TOILET TRIVIA

According to the website Useless Information:

44% of people wipe from front to back behind their backs.
60% of people look at the paper after they wipe.
50% have wiped with leaves.
8% have wiped with their hands.

WHEN THE BALL DROPS
Great Stories in Diarrhea

at the moment of reckoning,

when there is no tomorrow or yesterday,

when the cork comes out of the bottle...

...the ball drops.

⚠ The Day Player ⚠

In my early days in Los Angeles, I frequently worked as what we in the motion picture industry call a "day player". I would be hired onto the lighting crew for days when they needed additional guys, or to cover a regular. People such as myself would come "play" for a day or two at a time, instead of working the entire show.

I had just come off a stint on the highly regarded production of *Leprechaun VI: Leprechaun Back 2 Tha Hood*. For those of you who know the series, VI was kind of a sequel to V (*Leprechaun In Tha Hood*), continuing its gangland narrative and following an opportunistic young hip-hop artist who—in a Faustian turn—sees fit to steal the Leprechaun's über-choice stash of four-leaf clover doobage. Needless to say, this unleashes the Leprechaun's wrath, forming the crux of the denouement. But that was yesterday.

Today, I set off to work on a green-screen music video at a little sound stage on Sunset Boulevard. I had brought along my friend Isaac, who had expressed interest in getting into film lighting work, no doubt enamored by my star-laden tales of working in Hollywood...

"I mean, that little guy was in Willow!"

We were glad to see that the sound stage was pretty small—shouldn't be a big deal... might even get home at a decent hour... I pictured the Leprechaun shining his luck down on us as we grabbed a quick coffee and a stale muffin and got to work.

Unlike many stages, where there are stairs or elevators up to the catwalks (and the so-called "perms"), this place has another system. There's an electric trolley with a hydraulic "scissor lift" that you load up with your gear. You then drive it over underneath the grid, raise it up to the upper level, climb over and dump the load into the perms—kind of a hassle, but beats carrying stuff up stairs. I introduce Isaac to some of the other guys and they get going on floor power while a sturdy guy named Omari (the Best Boy Electric) and I tackle the scissor lift.

We hoist the first load of cables up to the perms to power our "Sky Pans" and I began to sort them and distribute them around the grid, getting ready to tie them off and drop down the plugs. I'm leaning over to do this work and as I right myself, I am suddenly aware of a change in internal pressure. The ball is inflating.

I look down at the floor below through the gaps in the catwalk floor. Even before I am able to parse the messages from my guts I am quite aware of the fact that Omari and the escape vehicle are, by this point, long gone. I see him down below, where Isaac is handing him more cables.

I do the proverbial look-around. No stairs. No elevator. Not even a rickety wooden ladder. As my fellow ball-droppers know, sometimes the warning interval can be brief: suddenly, I'm pondering jumping. It's only like 20 feet, which in the moment seems quite doable.

"OMARI!!!!!!"

We'd only met that morning, but instantly he can tell there's something wrong in the perms. He drops the coil of cable he's counting, leaps into the scissor-lift and takes off, but I am far from safe.

While we've been working on lighting, the stage people have decided to give the green curved walls and floor a fresh coat of paint, starting right below me. What was once a direct path from our staging area to the perms is now cordoned off and covered in wet paint, forcing Omari to circumnavigate.

It's a race against my biological clock (anyone else tired of that term being used solely in reference to the impatient-to-be-pregnant women of the world?) and the race vehicle is old, orange, and running out of batteries. Scissor-lifts need to be charged every night, which is usually done but even then, the older the battery, the less charge it holds. So the race is on but it's happening at 1 MPH and it's like a 17-point turn to maneuver back to me. I watch him turn the front wheels, lurch backwards, reposition the wheels, roll forward, repeat. The peristaltic bowel metaphor is hard to ignore; the same circuitous undulation dances within me.

What would usually take six seconds is suddenly becoming a three minute drive and I can do the math: he's not going to be make it in time. I'm wondering how good of a barrier the gaps in the catwalk floor are going to be. Is it like a rowboat, where they swell with moisture, or is it like a sieve, where they merely strain out the bits?

Not wanting to deal with the answer and intuitively presaging my waterfall, I muster the foresight to tuck my pant cuffs into my socks, but with Omari only just beginning to extend the chassis skywards, the deluge arrives—instantly filling my pants. I'm fly-fishing and I've gone in over my chest waders. The left leg is inexplicably heavier than the right and on both sides the elastic in my socks is doing all it can to keep the levee intact. It is only thanks to this elastic that there wasn't an avalanche rained down from above onto the newly painted green canvas; Robin Hood's color palette resurrected. I think I managed to leave the perms mostly clean except for a couple of drips of plausible deniability; the dropping of the ball leads to some wishful thinking.

The scissor-lift arrives and while it's taking every ounce of strength I have to play it cool, I can't help but wonder how much of my goings-on above are known to Omari and the world below. He can tell I'm in bad shape, and somehow he helps me climb over the waist-high railing and clamber out across the abyss and onto the platform of the lift. By now my shoes are overflowing with a sock-filtered distillate and I can't imagine the lift or the ground below dodged the dribbles completely.

We arrive at ground level and I wood-walk straight for my car skipping eye contact with everyone and saying something like "Isaac I gotta run I'll call you" in a a single syllable. I leave my tools behind but swipe my red sweatshirt on the way out the door and lay it down on my driver's seat to protect the upholstery (which, delighted, worked!) and drive home, straight into the shower.

All this before 9am. My girlfriend was still in bed and very confused that I was home so early. "Go back to sleep," I told her and followed suit, preferring to give this day a second take.

Perhaps it was I not that opportunistic young hip-hop artist who entered into a Faustian pact with the devious green goblin-creature that is Los Angeles. Perhaps "Leprechaun's Revenge" was my recompense. —ABB

WHEN THE BALL DROPS
Great Stories in Diarrhea

at the moment of reckoning,

when there is no tomorrow or yesterday,

when the cork comes out of the bottle...

...the ball drops.

⚠ Elevator Action ⚠

It was a beautiful spring night in 1994. Nine friends and I, all seniors in high school at the time, spent the evening in New York City. We began the night at the Hard Rock Cafe for some dinner. It was pretty uneventful, although we did meet a group of high schools girls visiting from out of town. After finding out where the girls were staying, the guys and I made our way to Legz Diamond. For the uninitiated, Legz Diamond is a nudie bar in the heart of Times Square and, needless to say, a real classy establishment. We spent a couple of hours and a couple rolls of singles in the strip club. We then proceeded to the aforementioned girls' hotel, the Ameritania, conveniently located only a block or so away from Legz.

The hooligans and I made our way into the hotel elevator. Mind you, the elevator fit about eight people comfortably, and we were ten. We all got in, the door closed, and we pressed the button for the girls' floor. Our excitement and anticipation was building, so much so that one of my genius friends decided to jump in the air while the elevator was making its way up. As my friend hit the ground, the elevator instantly stopped—right in the middle of two floors. We first took turns berating my friend, then we pushed the emergency button to call for assistance. Minutes went by and there was no sign of help.

It started to get warmer and warmer in the elevator and the bickering began. We were able to pry the doors open, but all that proved was that we were stuck in between floors and there was no way out. There was a little opening for some air to come in from outside the elevator, and this would prove invaluable in a few minutes.

After we'd been stuck for another 30 minutes, one of my friends announced to the group that he needed to take a dump and he might not be able to hold it in. We told him to calm down, that help would be on its way shortly, and he'd be in a bathroom in no time. But as time went by and his face became a red, grimaced mask, it became obvious to one and all that he really might not be able to wait.

After about 45 minutes, he took off his button down shirt, and then his white undershirt. He insisted that he couldn't wait any longer and placed the undershirt on the floor. We yelled at him, urging him not to do what it looked like he was about to do. I must admit, I didn't think he could possibly go through with it.

But there he was, pulling down his pants and assuming a shitting position over the undershirt. We realized he was not fucking around and made one last collective plea for him to control himself, somehow, some way.

"I can't take it any more!" he shouted. "I have to shit and there's nothing any one can do about it."

At this, we all gathered close together, as far away from the shit scene as possible, and turned away. The next thing I knew, the elevator smelled like a shit grenade had just gone off. I turned back to see what my former friend had done and there it was: a heaping pile of poo sitting on top of his white undershirt. To his credit, it looked like it just came out of a Carvel soft serve ice cream machine.

Looking back now, that was really quite an impressive display of dumping ability. At the time, however, my other friends and I couldn't see the forest for the trees. We were not too pleased to say the least.

The heat in the elevator combined with the shit-filled undershirt made it impossible to breathe. The curses and obscenities that came out of our mouths were endless; we could not fathom how someone could do what he just did.

Then it got worse. With my head buried deep in my shirt trying to avoid the shit smell, I heard what sounded like the distinct sound of someone urinating. It couldn't be, could it? Oh yes it was. My friend figured while he was at it, why not finish the job and add some piss icing on his shit cake?

We must have spent at least another 30 minutes in that elevator, each of us taking turns breathing through the opening in the elevator door. It felt as if someone had dunked my head in a sink filled with diarrhea and just wouldn't let go.

Finally, the fire department arrived and pulled each of us out of the elevator one by one. After the last one of us exited the elevator of death, there was only one thing remaining, the shit-filled shirt. The poor firemen. None of us remained behind to see their reaction, which I'm sure would have been priceless. By the way, we did end up in the girls' hotel room for a couple of hours. A few of the guys managed to hook up with the out-of-owners. Unfortunately, I was not one of them, but the shitter was. —SS

TOILET TRIVIA

Toilets use more water than any other household appliance.

WHEN THE BALL DROPS
Great Stories in Diarrhea

at the moment of reckoning,
when there is no tomorrow or yesterday,
when the cork comes out of the bottle...
...the ball drops.

⚠ Jeff's Brother ⚠

My friend, for this story we will call him "Jeff," was watching his brother while his parents were at work. Or should I say, he was told to watch his brother while his parents were at work. The only thing Jeff watched was television, or his friends swimming, or his brother do stupid human tricks.

This brings me to my story. It was a hot summer day back in '83 and Jeff had a bunch of us over to swim. His brother, younger by three years and not much of a swimmer, would usually just hang out with all of us until one of us in the group would egg him on to do something stupid. For example, he might eat a bug or eat a dozen bananas—nothing really harmful, just gross kid stuff.

However, on this particular day, Jeff's brother took it upon himself to outdo himself.

Unbeknownst to us, as we were enjoying a beautiful sunny day in the pool, Jeff's brother was inside the house admiring his dad's new gumball machine that was filled with sugarless bubblegum. Instead of chewing the bubblegum, he decided to eat it. And eat it and eat it and eat it. In the end, approximately half the gumballs from the machine were in his stomach.

After a couple of hours, he ventured outside and, of course, we had to mess with him. We dared him to drink a jar of pickle juice and, being the trooper he was, he did it. Now I am not a chemist, but apparently there must be some sort of nuclear reaction when you mix pickle juice and sugarless bubblegum. I will get to that shortly.

Jeff's dad arrived home from work about an hour later. He told his sons he needed to go the store and asked if they wanted to go with him. They said yes, got dressed, and off they went. At this time, I feel obligated to remind you, dear readers, that the year was 1983 and society was still in an awkward state of dressing itself. For some reason, Jeff's dad let his younger brother dress up in shorts, a t-shirt, a cowboy hat, and cowboy boots. Why do I remember this so specifically? All will be revealed.

I have heard that younger children sometimes have a hard time accepting the fact that they have to drop wolf bait. Jeff's younger brother was one these kids to the extreme. As they were shopping, Jeff could hear his younger brothers' stomach churning. His dad asked his youngest son if he had to go to the bathroom, and he replied "no." After three more "movements," Jeff's brother finally got the hint that he was at DEFCON 1 and there was no turning back. He had to go. He told his dad and off he went.

About fifteen minutes later, Jeff's dad began to worry about where his youngest son was, so he told Jeff to go find his brother. As soon as Jeff made the turn out of the aisle, he noticed something on the floor. It started off as small drops, than the drops got bigger and bigger as he got closer to the bathroom. Jeff was about to see something beyond imagination. As he entered the bathroom, there were puddles of pudding on the floor. Only this wasn't no Jell-O Brand and you sure didn't want to be eating it. He saw his brother's boots in the stall, only he was not wearing them. The smell was ungodly rotten. He heard what he thought was crying and asked his brother if he was OK. No response. Again, Jeff asked his brother if he was OK but heard no answer. Finally, Jeff's brother opened the door to the stall. Jeff described the scene this way: "my brother had painted himself and the entire stall with crap. The load had not only filled his pants, but had run down and filled up his cowboy boots to the point of overflow—hence the little trail to the bathroom. Shit had also gotten on his shirt, so when tried to take it off, he had smeared it all over his back and head. In the meantime, he had removed his hat and placed it on the ground. When he went to take off his boots, he filled up the hat like a bowl of chili.

As all of this is happening, he got so frustrated that he started to fling his shirt around, causing poop spackle to gather all over the stall walls. It looked like he was covered in mud and playing in it. Let's just say they were probably tempted to call in the HAZMAT team for this clean up. Either that, or old Earl was getting hazardous duty pay. Anyway, Jeff was terrified and he ran out of the bathroom to find his father. He described the scene, and his dad rushed to the bathroom, only to see now that his youngest son was standing naked, except for all the crap on his body, trying in vain to clean up the debris on the walls by wiping it with toilet paper. Despite his good intentions, all he was doing was evening out the first coat on the wall.

Jeff's dad immediately told Jeff to go out in the store and find some underwear, shorts, and a t-shirt for his brother. Dad threw out all the soiled clothes and bathed his youngest son in the sink. Jeff returned with the clothes, they changed his brother into his new duds, and started walking towards the checkout. As they turned the aisle to go up front, Jeff glanced back at the bathroom only to see three people standing outside covering their noses in shock. He claimed that one of them puked, but that detail was added years later so most likely it was an exaggeration. But anything is possible.

The moral of this story? Don't keep sugarless bubble gum in your house. Or let Jeff watch your kids. . . —TL

WHEN THE BALL DROPS
Great Stories in Diarrhea

at the moment of reckoning,

when there is no tomorrow or yesterday,

when the cork comes out of the bottle...

...the ball drops.

⚠ **The real *Real World*** ⚠

Let me just preface this story by stating what should be obvious: shitting one's pants is never exactly a proud moment. But I did once have a public diarrhea experience where I was able to show my mettle and impress my husband.

Before I get to the story itself, I must confess that I am a huge fan of reality TV. Not so much the bug eating, race-around-the-world kind of stuff, but I do love any stupid show that records the embarrassing behavior of twenty-somethings in a "way too hip" house that they could never afford under normal circumstances. Did I mention I'm about 10 or so years older than any of the target demographics for all of these shows? I guess not. Anyway, on with the story . . .

It was a beautiful spring night and I was on a juice diet. OK, truth be told, it was a modified juice diet—no food, a little juice...lots of alcohol. My husband and I were out in Manhattan at our local watering hole, having a few drinks and talking to the bartender, when I noticed a photo shoot going on in the back room. This being New York, things like this are going on constantly, so it barely registered in my head. Then one of the "models" walked to the bar and ordered a drink. I recognized him but couldn't quite place him. Then the second "model" approached and it hit me. These were kids from *The Real World*!! My husband had no idea who they were because he only watches age-appropriate TV. But I was immediately star struck (though I'll admit I'm using the term "star" loosely).

Eventually the photo shoot moved to our end of the bar and the regulars (including myself) start asking some benign questions about the shoot—OK, we were really just busting the kids' balls. I pointed out a little too loudly that the puppy in one of the shots looked a lot better than his co-star "model." The guy turned red and was clearly pissed at me for mocking him in front of his friends but had no response. After an hour or so, my husband and I moved on to another location to meet friends.

Several hours, and many more cocktails later, we were heading back home. As I stepped off the curb, only two blocks from our apartment, I experienced what I can only describe as spontaneous anal leakage (pure liquid). This was the first time that had ever happened to me. My first physical reaction was to tighten every muscle in the lower half of my body in an effort to prevent further ass leaking. I said to my husband, "You are not going to believe what just happened."

He was completely oblivious. "I just shit my pants. . .and here's the kicker-I'm wearing a thong." Now, as you may or may not know, a thong does not provide the coverage area nor the absorbency that normal, ass-covering underwear does.

Unable to even climb the four flights of stairs to my apartment, I suggested we duck into a different quiet pub directly across the street for a quick clean up mission. As I opened the door, much to my dismay, I was immediately faced with about 30 *Real World* cast members from different seasons. I, of course, recognized all of them.

I attempted to slip into the ladies' room unnoticed, but alas, I was the one recognized in this room full of D-list stars. It was none other than the "model" from the earlier photo shoot! He proceeded to call me over to "confront" me for embarrassing him in front of his fellow cast members. I will say, however, his wit had not quickened in the few hours since our last meeting (thank God). I quickly put him back in his place by making some joke about his general cluelessness.

I was terrified the whole time that as soon as I walked away the assembled crowd would see my secret shame through the back of my white capris. But luckily for me, no one seemed to see a thing. I went to the bathroom and the damage was nowhere near as bad as I expected. The leak had magically been contained by a one-inch strip of fabric. Here, I must officially declare the designers of Vanity Fair lingerie to be geniuses as I was able to easily clean up for the short trip home.

I saw my husband outside and I told him the whole story of how I put the "model" back in his place for the second time that night.

"I saw. Did he tell you that you smelled like shit? I can't believe you were talking to him with a load of shit in your pants!"

To this day, I'm not sure if he was disgusted or impressed. But I choose to believe the latter. —SM

 TOILET TRIVIA

A high-powered public restroom toilet can have a splash radius as far as 20 feet.

THE DOODIE LOG

THE DOODIE LOG

Stool Sample Or How to fill in Your Log

Date:

November 24, 2008

Name:

Johnny Pluntfarb

Number of Stools:

3

Length of Stools:

3 inches, 4 inches (broke in half), 2 one inch stragglers.

Girth:

Larger stools .75 inches diameter.

Shape:

Larger stools - slight arch, mostly straight. 2 small pebbles.

Color:

Park bench brown

Odor:

Slight

Texture (as best you can tell):

Slight blackberry like compacted parts, smooth.

Ease of Exit:

Swam out like a fish being thrown back into the ocean.

Slight exertion on stragglers.

Clean-up:

Moderate. Significant first wipes.

Follow-ups for safety.

Recent Meals:

Chicken fajita; chips/salsa; ham sandwich

Thought about while going:

Need to find tenant for investment property;

what is Bull from "Night Court" doing now?

Additional Comments:

Apparent lack of digestion of some sort of pepper;

audible plopping with some splashback, need came

upon suddenly. Sat for an extra five minutes just because.

THE DOODIE LOG

Date:

_____

Name:

_____

Number of Stools:

_____

Length of Stools:

_____

Girth:

_____

Shape:

_____

Color:

_____

Odor:

_____

Texture (as best you can tell):

_____

Ease of Exit:

_____

_____

Clean-up:

_____

_____

Recent Meals:

_____

_____

Thought about while going:

_____

_____

Additional Comments:

_____

_____

_____

THE DOODIE LOG

Date:

_____

Name:

_____

Number of Stools:

_____

Length of Stools:

_____

Girth:

_____

Shape:

_____

Color:

_____

Odor:

_____

Texture (as best you can tell):

_____

Ease of Exit:

_____

_____

Clean-up:

_____

_____

Recent Meals:

_____

_____

Thought about while going:

_____

_____

Additional Comments:

_____

_____

_____

THE DOODIE LOG

Date:

_____

Name:

_____

Number of Stools:

_____

Length of Stools:

_____

Girth:

_____

Shape:

_____

Color:

_____

Odor:

_____

Texture (as best you can tell):

_____

Ease of Exit:

_____

_____

Clean-up:

_____

_____

Recent Meals:

_____

_____

Thought about while going:

_____

_____

Additional Comments:

_____

_____

_____

THE DOODIE LOG

Date:

_____

Name:

_____

Number of Stools:

_____

Length of Stools:

_____

Girth:

_____

Shape:

_____

Color:

_____

Odor:

_____

Texture (as best you can tell):

_____

Ease of Exit:

_____

_____

Clean-up:

_____

_____

Recent Meals:

_____

_____

Thought about while going:

_____

_____

Additional Comments:

_____

_____

_____

THE DOODIE LOG

Date:

_____

Name:

_____

Number of Stools:

_____

Length of Stools:

_____

Girth:

_____

Shape:

_____

Color:

_____

Odor:

_____

Texture (as best you can tell):

_____

Ease of Exit:

_____

_____

Clean-up:

_____

_____

Recent Meals:

_____

_____

Thought about while going:

_____

_____

Additional Comments:

_____

_____

_____

THE DOODIE LOG

Date:

_____

Name:

_____

Number of Stools:

_____

Length of Stools:

_____

Girth:

_____

Shape:

_____

Color:

_____

Odor:

_____

Texture (as best you can tell):

_____

Ease of Exit:

_____

_____

Clean-up:

_____

_____

Recent Meals:

_____

_____

Thought about while going:

_____

_____

Additional Comments:

_____

_____

_____

THE DOODIE LOG

Date:

_____

Name:

_____

Number of Stools:

_____

Length of Stools:

_____

Girth:

_____

Shape:

_____

Color:

_____

Odor:

_____

Texture (as best you can tell):

_____

Ease of Exit:

_____

_____

Clean-up:

_____

_____

Recent Meals:

_____

_____

Thought about while going:

_____

_____

Additional Comments:

_____

_____

_____

THE DOODIE LOG

Date:

_____

Name:

_____

Number of Stools:

_____

Length of Stools:

_____

Girth:

_____

Shape:

_____

Color:

_____

Odor:

_____

Texture (as best you can tell):

_____

Ease of Exit:

_____

_____

Clean-up:

_____

_____

Recent Meals:

_____

_____

Thought about while going:

_____

_____

Additional Comments:

_____

_____

_____

THE DOODIE LOG

Date:

_____

Name:

_____

Number of Stools:

_____

Length of Stools:

_____

Girth:

_____

Shape:

_____

Color:

_____

Odor:

_____

Texture (as best you can tell):

_____

Ease of Exit:

_____

_____

Clean-up:

_____

_____

Recent Meals:

_____

_____

Thought about while going:

_____

_____

Additional Comments:

_____

_____

_____

THE DOODIE LOG

Date:

_____

Name:

_____

Number of Stools:

_____

Length of Stools:

_____

Girth:

_____

Shape:

_____

Color:

_____

Odor:

_____

Texture (as best you can tell):

_____

Ease of Exit:

_____

_____

Clean-up:

_____

_____

Recent Meals:

_____

_____

Thought about while going:

_____

_____

Additional Comments:

_____

_____

_____

THE DOODIE LOG

Date:

_____

Name:

_____

Number of Stools:

_____

Length of Stools:

_____

Girth:

_____

Shape:

_____

Color:

_____

Odor:

_____

Texture (as best you can tell):

_____

Ease of Exit:

_____

_____

Clean-up:

_____

_____

Recent Meals:

_____

_____

Thought about while going:

_____

_____

Additional Comments:

_____

_____

_____

THE DOODIE LOG

Date:

_____

Name:

_____

Number of Stools:

_____

Length of Stools:

_____

Girth:

_____

Shape:

_____

Color:

_____

Odor:

_____

Texture (as best you can tell):

_____

Ease of Exit:

_____

_____

Clean-up:

_____

_____

Recent Meals:

_____

_____

Thought about while going:

_____

_____

Additional Comments:

_____

_____

_____

THE DOODIE LOG

Date:

_____

Name:

_____

Number of Stools:

_____

Length of Stools:

_____

Girth:

_____

Shape:

_____

Color:

_____

Odor:

_____

Texture (as best you can tell):

_____

Ease of Exit:

_____

_____

Clean-up:

_____

_____

Recent Meals:

_____

_____

Thought about while going:

_____

_____

Additional Comments:

_____

_____

_____

THE DOODIE LOG

Date:

_____

Name:

_____

Number of Stools:

_____

Length of Stools:

_____

Girth:

_____

Shape:

_____

Color:

_____

Odor:

_____

Texture (as best you can tell):

_____

Ease of Exit:

_____

_____

Clean-up:

_____

_____

Recent Meals:

_____

_____

Thought about while going:

_____

_____

Additional Comments:

_____

_____

_____

THE DOODIE LOG

Date:

_____

Name:

_____

Number of Stools:

_____

Length of Stools:

_____

Girth:

_____

Shape:

_____

Color:

_____

Odor:

_____

Texture (as best you can tell):

_____

Ease of Exit:

_____

_____

Clean-up:

_____

_____

Recent Meals:

_____

_____

Thought about while going:

_____

_____

Additional Comments:

_____

_____

_____

EMERGENCY TOILET PAPER

Appendix: Emergency Toilet Paper

In event of emergency, tear along dotted line. In order to minimize discomfort, half crumple the page. Crumpling too much will create too many harsh folds. Not crumpling enough will put you at risks of paper cuts in bad places. Dab. Do not wipe too hard.

- -

- -

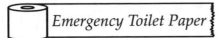*Emergency Toilet Paper*

- -

- -

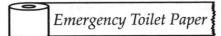

Emergency Toilet Paper

- -

- -

Emergency Toilet Paper

- -

- -

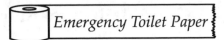

Emergency Toilet Paper

Got a Good Bathroom Story?

Don't be shy, be a part of the movement.

Share your very own When The Ball Drops story (aka the Diarrhea Monologues) with the world. We here at Seven Footer Press are in the process of collecting and archiving all of the world's greatest stories of self-defecation (or close calls).

While we can't offer any monetary compensation, just think of the joy that being published in our next book will engender among your friends, family and colleagues. Immortality awaits, so start typing.

Please send your submissions to:

Seven Footer Press
276 Fifth Ave., Suite 301
New York, NY 10001
Attn: When the Ball Drops

Or email to: **whentheballdrops@sevenfooter.com**

www.sevenfooter.com